# Qualitative HCI Research:

*Going Behind the Scenes*

# Synthesis Lectures on Human-Centered Informatics

## Editor
**John M. Carroll**, *Penn State University*

Human-Centered Informatics (HCI) is the intersection of the cultural, the social, the cognitive, and the aesthetic with computing and information technology. It encompasses a huge range of issues, theories, technologies, designs, tools, environments, and human experiences in knowledge work, recreation and leisure activity, teaching and learning, and the potpourri of everyday life. The series publishes state-of-the-art syntheses, case studies, and tutorials in key areas. It shares the focus of leading international conferences in HCI.

July 2013

Translating Euclid: Designing a Human-Centered Mathematics
Gerry Stahl
April 2013

Adaptive Interaction: A Utility Maximisation Approach to Understanding Human Interaction
with Technology
Stephen J. Payne and Andrew Howes
March 2013

Making Claims: Knowledge Design, Capture, and Sharing in HCI
D. Scott McCrickard
June 2012

HCI Theory: Classical, Modern, and Contemporary
Yvonne Rogers
May 2012

Activity Theory in HCI: Fundamentals and Reflections
Victor Kaptelinin and Bonnie Nardi
April 2012

Conceptual Models: Core to Good Design
Jeff Johnson and Austin Henderson
November 2011

Geographical Design: Spatial Cognition and Geographical Information Science
Stephen C. Hirtle
March 2011

User-Centered Agile Methods
Hugh Beyer
2010

Experience-Centered Design: Designers, Users, and Communities in Dialogue
Peter Wright and John McCarthy
2010

Experience Design: Technology for All the Right Reasons
Marc Hassenzahl
2010

Qualitative HCI Research: Going Behind the Scenes
Ann Blandford, Dominic Furniss, and Stephann Makri
www.morganclaypool.com

ISBN: 9781627057592 print
ISBN: 9781627057608 ebook

DOI 10.2200/S00706ED1V01Y201602HCI034

A Publication in the Morgan & Claypool Publishers series
*SYNTHESIS LECTURES ON HUMAN-CENTERED INFORMATICS #34*
Series Editors: John M. Carroll, Penn State University

Series ISSN 1946-7680 Print     1946-7699 Electronic

# Qualitative HCI Research:

## *Going Behind the Scenes*

**Ann Blandford**
University College London
**Dominic Furniss**
University College London
**Stephann Makri**
City University London

*SYNTHESIS LECTURES ON HUMAN–CENTERED INFORMATICS #34*

MORGAN & CLAYPOOL PUBLISHERS

## ABSTRACT

Human–Computer Interaction (HCI) addresses problems of interaction design: understanding user needs to inform design, delivering novel designs that meet user needs, and evaluating new and existing designs to determine their success in meeting user needs. Qualitative methods have an essential role to play in this enterprise, particularly in understanding user needs and behaviours and evaluating situated use of technology. Qualitative methods allow HCI researchers to ask questions where the answers are more complex and interesting than "true" or "false," and may also be unexpected. In this lecture, we draw on the analogy of making a documentary film to discuss important issues in qualitative HCI research: historically, films were presented as finished products, giving the viewer little insight into the production process; more recently, there has been a trend to go behind the scenes to expose some of the painstaking work that went into creating the final cut. Similarly, in qualitative research, the essential work behind the scenes is rarely discussed. There are many "how to" guides for particular methods, but few texts that start with the purpose of a study and then discuss the important details of how to select a suitable method, how to adapt it to fit the study context, or how to deal with unexpected challenges that arise. We address this gap by presenting a repertoire of qualitative techniques for understanding user needs, practices and experiences with technology for the purpose of informing design. We also discuss practical considerations such as tactics for recruiting participants and ways of getting started when faced with a pile of interview transcripts. Our particular focus is on semi-structured qualitative studies, which occupy a space between ethnography and surveys—typically involving observations, interviews and similar methods for data gathering, and methods of analysis based on systematic coding of data. Just as a documentary team faces challenges that often go unreported when arranging expeditions or interviews and gathering and editing footage within time and budget constraints, so the qualitative research team faces challenges in obtaining ethical clearance, recruiting participants, analysing data, choosing how and what to report, etc. We present illustrative examples drawn from prior experience to bring to life the purpose, planning and practical considerations of doing qualitative studies for interaction design. We include takeaway checklists for planning, conducting, reporting and evaluating semi-structured qualitative studies.

## KEYWORDS

qualitative methods, QDA, grounded theory, Thematic Analysis, Ethnography, Observational studies, interview studies

# Contents

# Acknowledgments

This book owes its existence to the many students and researchers we have worked with over the years. It builds on an earlier chapter on Semi-Structured Qualitative Methods published by the Interaction Design Foundation (Blandford, 2014), and a few sentences from that text may have made it through into this one unscathed.

We cannot list everyone who has shaped and challenged our thinking about qualitative methods: there are too many, and we would be sure to forget someone important. We thank you all. Suzanne Amos, Ellie Burgess, Imogen Lyons, Nikki Newhouse, Olga Perski, Sheila Pontis and Kathy Stawarz gave constructive feedback on an earlier draft of this text; many thanks! Paul Cairns, Marc Hassenzahl, Jesper Kjeldskov, Helena Mentis and Mark Perry have made excellent suggestions for improving this manuscript; we have addressed as many as possible of their recommendations, but remaining limitations are our responsibility. Emily Blandford and Smaragda Magou have delivered illustrations that surpass our rather limited graphic design skills. Aisling O'Kane and Atish Rajkomar have given permission to include photographs from studies led by them. Our research has been funded by EPSRC, ESRC, MRC, SSHRC and NIHR.

# Preface

The motivation for writing this book came from several different directions. The key driver was that there has not been a good text that we could direct our students to that resonates with their interests and the problems they are addressing. There are some excellent texts from the social sciences and from healthcare, but they do not deal with problems of interaction design, user requirements or user experience when interacting with technology. Conversely, there are many excellent HCI texts that focus on observation, task analysis or research methods, but none that focus specifically on qualitative methods. We intend that this book should plug that gap.

A second motivation comes from the perennial question or challenge: what constitutes quality in qualitative HCI research? Is it even research? We should raise the quality of the discourse on what constitutes valid, reliable and valuable qualitative research in HCI. We should also raise the quality of that research, so that it becomes more valuable and has greater integrity.

We have chosen to draw on the analogy of going behind the scenes when making a documentary. Our main sources of inspiration for this have been Dom's experience of making short films to communicate our research and Ann's delight at watching "behind the scenes" footage on the making of wildlife documentaries (BBC, 2014). Of course, a qualitative study is expected to have a scientific rigour that is not expected of many documentaries, but they both share issues in gathering data, creating a narrative and representing some aspect of reality to inform an audience. Our focus on going behind the scenes means that we draw a lot on our own experiences, because we know what went on behind the scenes in our studies. So long as there is little tradition of reporting these details, that information is not accessible for other researchers' projects, and it is difficult to be reflective about the work of others when you don't have the insider knowledge. So we hope this book will encourage you to consider taking readers of your own research "behind the scenes"—providing them with useful detail and justification on what you did and why.

In this book, we are pre-supposing a good general knowledge of HCI, but less detailed knowledge of qualitative methods. Our primary audience is Master's and Ph.D. students in HCI and related areas who are planning their individual projects. Other audiences include HCI practitioners who are planning in-depth studies, or people with a background in qualitative methods but who are new to HCI. We hope that this book will help you design and conduct excellent qualitative HCI studies.

Ann Blandford, Dominic Furniss and Stephann Makri, February 2016

# Glossary

The following abbreviations are used in this book:

| | |
|---|---|
| DCog | Distributed Cognition |
| DiCoT | Distributed Cognition for Teamwork |
| GT | Grounded Theory |
| HCI | Human–Computer Interaction |
| QDA | Qualitative Data Analysis |
| SSQS | Semi-Structured Qualitative Study |
| TA | Thematic Analysis |

# CHAPTER 1

# Introduction

*BEHIND THE SCENES*

Qualitative methods play an important role in Human–Computer Interaction (HCI): in requirements gathering, in acquiring an understanding of the situations in which technology is used and might be used and in evaluating how technologies are used in practice. Although there are scores of texts on qualitative methods in the social sciences, there are surprisingly few in HCI. The concerns of HCI are somewhat different from those of the social sciences, with a focus on technology use for informing the design of interactive systems, rather than on social phenomena between individuals, in organisations and in  society more generally. Our aim in this book is to take you behind the scenes, to give guidance on how to plan, conduct and report qualitative studies in HCI. Throughout, we draw on the metaphor of making a documentary to bring to life important issues, and to make producing something a more tangible part of the activity. Going behind the scenes allows us to examine important considerations for qualitative research in the field of HCI that have seldom been discussed elsewhere.

The emphasis we place on different topics is inevitably colored by our own experiences. Our research has been in two main areas: healthcare technologies (e.g., Furniss et al., 2015; Hsu and Blandford, 2014; Rajkomar et al., 2015) and interacting with information (e.g., Blandford and Attfield, 2010; Makri et al., 2008a; Makri and Warwick, 2010). The first of these brings challenges, particularly in engaging with patients and dealing with sensitive issues within complex healthcare processes. The second brings a different kind of challenge: that interacting with information is often not the primary focus of someone's activity; it is a secondary activity that they barely notice, so gathering useful and reliable information about users' interactions can be difficult. Using these and other experiences, we review challenges and provide advice for designing and conducting qualitative HCI research.

## 1.1 AN OVERVIEW OF QUALITATIVE APPROACHES AND METHODS IN HCI

There are many, many approaches and methods for qualitative research. Some of them have names, such as Ethnography, Contextual Inquiry, Focus Groups, Grounded Theory, Interpretive Phenomenological Analysis, Discourse Analysis or Thematic Analysis; others do not. Some—such as

Contextual Inquiry and Grounded Theory—are widely used in HCI, while others—such as Interpretive Phenomenological Analysis and Discourse Analysis—are not; we focus on the more widely used methods and approaches in this book. Some of these names have precise meanings; others are often used as generic descriptors of qualitative research. For example, Grounded Theory (GT) has been described as a "bumper sticker" (Bryman and Burgess, 1994) to cover a broad range of qualitative approaches, even though there are strong principles underpinning GT proper. This makes

it particularly important for HCI researchers to be open and transparent when explaining and justifying the qualitative approaches they have adopted. When writing up an approach, it is essential for researchers to explain in detail what they did and why, giving reasons for adopting, adapting or combining particular established approaches.

Denzin and Lincoln (2011) discuss a research process in terms of five phases, or levels of activity. The first phase is the researcher—you!—who comes to the study with their individual history, experiences, values and understanding; the researcher shapes the research, and should be aware of the role they are playing in the research.

The second phase is the research paradigm. In Chapter 6, we discuss research paradigms in terms of quantitative and qualitative approaches that are widely used in HCI. In brief: quantitative research is most commonly applied to test pre-determined hypotheses, whereas qualitative approaches aim to describe and explain phenomena in a rich, often exploratory, way. Denzin and Lincoln (2011) identify four major paradigms for qualitative research: positivist and post-positivist; constructivist-interpretive; critical (Marxist, emancipatory); and feminist-poststructural. Given the aims of HCI studies, focusing on the design and use of interactive technologies, qualitative HCI research generally fits within the first two of these paradigms, and this book focuses on the constructivist-interpretive paradigm. This paradigm assumes a subjective reality that is shaped by the interpretations of researchers and study participants. This can feel uncomfortable at first, particularly to those who have been brought up in a classic scientific paradigm where it is assumed that there is an objective reality "out there" and that the role of research is to establish what it is. This book is intended to provide tools and techniques to conduct high quality interpretive qualitative HCI research.

Denzin and Lincoln (2011) label their third phase "research strategies." This is the phase that focuses on the strategy for addressing the research question or purpose of the study. Their list of strategies includes several that are commonly used in HCI, including ethnography, participant observation, ethnomethodology and GT. We discuss these approaches in Chapter 6, after discussing the particular methods that make up a study (Chapters 4 and 5).

Their fourth phase is "methods of collection and analysis." They include interviewing, observation, autoethnography and focus groups as data collection methods; to this list, we add think-aloud as a technique that is particular to HCI (Chapter 4). We separate out analysis (Chapter 5), focusing particularly on Thematic Analysis (Braun and Clarke, 2006) as a technique for data analysis that is widely used in HCI.

The final phase according to Denzin and Lincoln (2011) is that of interpretation and evaluation. The questions in this phase are broadly: what can be learned from this study, how confident can we be in the findings and how might they be reported? In this book, we present this in terms of reporting the study (Chapter 7) and delivering the highest possible quality research (Chapter 8).

## 1.2 THE SPACE OF INTERPRETIVE QUALITATIVE STUDIES IN HCI

There are several important dimensions on which qualitative studies in HCI vary:

- **The focus of the study:** Qualitative studies in HCI, by definition, focus on current or future technology design and use. But there are still many possible questions that the study might address—e.g., "how does our new design compare with our competitor's design?" or "what are the privacy implications of introducing this new technology?"

- **Who provides the data:** Most studies involve the current or intended future users of the system of interest. Occasionally it is necessary to work with surrogate users—e.g., when real users are too busy to take part, or too expensive to recruit. Many studies also involve stakeholders in the system, such as domain experts who understand at least some of the users' technology needs. In healthcare, for example, medical practitioners might provide input on system functionality they believe their patients need.

- **Where the data is gathered:** For many studies, particularly observational ones, it is important to do the data gathering in the "field"—i.e., in the real world, where the technology will be used in practice. But interviews may be conducted away from the situation of use, and think-aloud studies that focus on the individual's interaction with a specific system often take place in controlled ("laboratory") settings.

- **How the data is gathered:** Most studies gather data through observation, interviews, focus groups, or diaries. Some studies use existing data such as incident reports, product reviews or system documentation.

- **How the study is structured:** Some studies have a clear stepwise structure, from devising research questions, to gathering data, to counting responses and producing results; others are more exploratory and iterative, which can include interleaving data gathering and analysis, as they refocus questions and find more meaning as they engage with the data. This is discussed in more detail in Chapter 6.

- **The relationship between the analyst and the data:** Some studies presume an objective reality to be "out there," and so two independent people can analyse the same data and discover the same conclusion; other studies recognise the role of the researcher in shaping the analysis and creating a narrative. We discuss positivist and interpretivist traditions that underlie these positions in more detail in Chapter 6. Throughout this book, we focus primarily on the interpretivist tradition.

This makes it sound as if there is enormous scope for variability. In practice, every study needs to be coherent: the approaches to gathering and analysing data need to be well suited to the research question, as discussed in more detail below.

In the following chapters, we expand on these themes to help you plan, conduct and report on your qualitative HCI study. Planning a study can seem overwhelming at first, but a focus on the purpose of the study, together with the courage to commit to early writing and to just getting on with things, can quickly make things seem more manageable.

In this book, we use the term "Semi-Structured Qualitative Study" (SSQS) to talk about the kinds of studies that are most commonly conducted in HCI. This term draws on the analogy of the semi-structured interview: that there is structure to give accountability and rigour while also creating space for exploring important avenues that are discovered through the process of doing the study. SSQSs occupy territory between studies that are based primarily on the analyst reporting their understanding of a situation in a free and unstructured manner and studies that are very structured in their approach and analyses. Our main reason for introducing this term is to add clarity to this area and to succinctly describe the kinds of study that are the focus of this text. It covers several different detailed approaches to qualitative studies in HCI. The key commonalities across these studies is that they have some clear structure that can be externalised.

## 1.3    OVERVIEW OF TOPICS

We found it difficult to choose an order for topics in this book, because everything is related to everything else. You cannot plan a study until you have some sense of what is and is not possible given the resources, constraints and context of that study. These considerations will include many factors such as who you can recruit and the intended size and scope of the project. Drawing on our film analogy: a major studio film is normally put together by many people working as a team, and each has an important role; however, independent films and documentaries are made on much lower budgets and can sometimes involve just one person doing the work. Documentaries do not need to be full feature length but can be short forays into a topic of interest. Qualitative studies can also differ in size and scope but the typical qualitative HCI study has a very small team (often only one or two people) and they have to play multiple roles—as producer, director, editor, etc.

The producer is involved in a lot of work in terms of the finances and contracts behind the film before any work begins, and then the film distribution once it has been created. Securing finances to realise a project can be difficult. In terms of research, these activities are likely to have been done by the project's Principal Investigator or your supervisor prior to any work on the project. We do not include those phases here but they are often key to making research possible.

The first role we consider is that of the director, who directs the making of the film and is responsible for achieving an artistic vision within budget: being creative to deliver a high quality product while also working with the available resources and constraints. Documentaries with human subjects may also include ethical considerations. In Chapter 2, we discuss the overall planning of a project, including the management of ethics and informed consent in studies.

A documentary relies on the footage it gathers of its subjects, e.g., this could be revealing interviews with key witnesses, capturing intimate behaviours of families or filming large mammals on the savannah. A scout might help find a location, and local guides might introduce suitable human participants, as part of pre-production for the film. Similarly, the quality of an HCI study can stand or fall on the data that is gathered which, in turn, depends heavily on the recruitment of participants to the study. In Chapter 3, we discuss sampling strategies and recruiting participants.

Of course the camera crew and sound technicians play a critical role in gathering footage under direction of the director. Capturing good quality data is essential, unless you are working with archive footage in which case you need to source it and review its quality. In Chapter 4, we discuss techniques for gathering data, including approaches to observation, interviewing, and getting participants to provide their own data (e.g., by keeping a diary).

The role of the editor becomes important at the point where the raw footage is selected, cut and joined together to create a coherent and compelling narrative that is faithful to the situation being documented. The editor might put the film together to highlight compelling themes that draw the viewer in or help them understand the topic in a new way. Just as the role of the editor is central to the quality of a documentary, so analysis is fundamental to the quality of a qualitative study. Approaches to analysis are discussed in Chapter 5.

Just as there are many different practices for putting together a documentary film, so there are many different approaches to qualitative research. We allude to many of these differences throughout the book, and in Chapter 6 we explicitly discuss different approaches, including Contextual Inquiry, ethnomethodology, GT and mixed methods approaches.

The final step of editing is creating the final cut, the finished film that is ready for viewing. The reporting should be credible (making it clear what the quality and limitations of the work are) while also being engaging. In Chapter 7, we discuss ways of reporting findings from a qualitative study.

For stakeholders in the production, the story does not end the moment the film is released. The film will be viewed, assessed and critically reviewed. Similarly, the report of a qualitative study will be assessed (e.g., the dissertation will be marked, the paper reviewed or the client report assessed by the client). In Chapter 8, we discuss the thorny question of how to evaluate qualitative research. This includes issues like validity, transferability and generalisability; different forms of triangulation; creativity and insight. Although Chapter 8 comes near the end, the issues are ones that should be considered from the outset, in the planning and conduct of the study.

This is a short book, where we present an overview of topics. However, we hope that you will enjoy your forays into qualitative HCI research and will want to learn more. In the final chapter, we summarise resources for going further.

Figure 1.1: Documentary films are different from fictional films in that they aim to present and document some aspects of life and reality, and further our understanding of their chosen subject. Like qualitative research, there are interesting questions about the techniques, practices and processes of representing facts while engaging and informing an audience. We go behind the scenes in this book to explore these issues.

CHAPTER   2

# Planning a Study

## *THE DIRECTOR'S WORK*

The art of devising any study is to match up what you are trying to achieve with the methods and resources at your disposal. While the film director may have a fairly blank canvas to work with, HCI is often about addressing pressing, practical problems or understanding future user needs. So a good place to start is with the purpose of a study.

Incidentally, most texts on qualitative methods do not start with the purpose: they typically start with a method, and then summarise (or leave the reader to infer) what that method is suitable for. We are taking a purpose-focused approach. From this perspective, the choice and application of an approach or technique are not right or wrong, but they are more or less well suited to the purpose of the study, and the aim is to select and adapt methods to be as good as possible for addressing that purpose. In Tables 2.1 and 2.2, we summarise some of the key features of the techniques and approaches covered in this book (see Chapters 4 and 6).

HCI is often problem-focused, delivering socio-technical solutions to identified user needs. Within this, there are two obvious roles for Semi-Structured Qualitative Studies (SSQSs): understanding current needs and practices and evaluating the effects of new technologies in practice. The typical interest is in how to understand the world in terms that are useful for interaction design. This can often demand a "bricolage" approach to study design, adopting and adapting methods to fit the constraints of a particular situation. On the one hand this makes it possible to address the most pressing problems or questions; on the other, the researcher is continually having to learn new skills, and be open to new possibilities. Experience with qualitative projects and techniques will bring a maturity that will make these possibilities and adaptations easier to handle.

**Table 2.1:** Key features of techniques

| Techniques | Features | Suited for | Considerations |
|---|---|---|---|
| Observation | Observing people working (or performing other activities) and interacting with technologies | Gaining an understanding of what people really do in practice | Without complementary interviews, it can be difficult to make sense of what is observed |
| Think-Aloud | Users talking through thoughts while interacting with a system or solving a problem | Understanding how people perceive and experience a system, and how they use it to support their work | Requires access to system. Data focuses on the system rather than the broader work context |
| Semi-Structured Interviews | Interviewing people about their work, their experiences of technology, their hopes for future technology, etc. | Gathering people's perceptions and experiences | People have difficulty reporting accurately on what they do |
| Focus Groups | Facilitating a group discussion, most commonly between people with similar backgrounds about the theme or technology of interest | Gathering perceptions and experiences, often with greater breadth but less depth than interviews | Focuses on perceptions rather than actions. Risk of "group think" unless carefully managed |
| Diary Studies | Participants maintain a diary of relevant actions, experiences or thoughts | Longitudinal data gathering that is situated in the context of use | May be fairly superficial unless participants have a high level of commitment |
| Autoethnography | Researcher participates in the intervention and maintains a diary of actions, experiences and reflections | Researcher gaining empathy with participants and with others who experience the intervention | Highly subjective, and probably not representative of the user population |
| Working with Existing Sources | Using existing sources (video, social media, audio, text…) as data for addressing the research problem | Building understanding based on background material | Data was generated for a different purpose and audience, so may not be directly suited to the current research question |

Table 2.2: Key features of approaches

| Approach | Features | Suited for | Considerations |
|---|---|---|---|
| Theory-Shaped Study | The design of data gathering and/or analysis is informed and constrained by the selected theory | Testing or extending theory; gaining insights into design or evaluation of system from the selected theoretical perspective | May overlook important considerations that are not covered by the theory |
| Ethnomethodology | Data gathering and analysis shaped by the ethnomethodological focus on how workers perform and "make sense" of their work | Gaining insights for design based on how people work and make sense of their work | May overlook important considerations that are not covered by the approach |
| Contextual Inquiry | Data gathering and preliminary analysis shaped by the constructs and questions of CI (information flow, artefact use, etc.) | Gaining insights for design based on information flow, how current artefacts are used, etc., within work | May overlook important considerations that are not covered by the CI models; not suited to mobile settings |
| Participant Observation | The researcher participates (to a greater or lesser extent) in the setting being studied | Getting immersed in the activity and experiencing something similar to what others experience in that situation | It is not always possible to participate meaningfully in the activity; requires reflexivity to understand one's own role in the situation |
| Action Research | Involves an intervention—e.g., introducing a new technology or process—and studying the effect of that intervention on work and user experience | Introducing innovations into the situation and understanding their effect on practice | Can be difficult to discern the effects that are attributable to the intervention; requires reflexivity |
| Grounded Theory | Involves interleaving data gathering (usually interviews) with analysis; focuses on systematically developing theory in its strongest form | Developing new theory from data | Depth of analysis may be disproportionate for small studies |

## 2.1    SO, YOU'VE GOT THIS GREAT IDEA OR BURNING QUESTION...

Every study has a purpose. As noted already, within HCI there are two main roles for qualitative studies: the first starts by trying to understand people's needs and the context within which a future technology might be used; and the second starts by assessing how well an existing technology is working and the effect that it is having on the people and the context. There are three common areas to focus on in HCI studies, as summarised below (see also Figure 2.1).

1. **How people exploit technologies to support cognition** (e.g., Hutchins 1995; Attfield and Blandford, 2011), or developing theories of emotion, cognition and interaction to inform design (e.g., McCarthy and Wright, 2005; Schneider et al., 2016).

2. **How a particular kind of technology shapes people's experiences** (e.g., Palen, 1999; Kindberg et al., 2005). This includes ways in which a new product changes attitudes and behaviours and how the design of the product might be adapted to better support people's needs and aspirations.

3. **The nature of particular "work"** (where "work" might be a leisure activity, paid work, home work or voluntary work), and how interactive technologies support or fail to support that work (e.g., Hartswood et al., 2003; Hughes et al., 1994; Mentis et al., 2013).

Figure 2.1: People use technology to achieve "work" (broadly conceived). The focus of HCI studies might be on or between any of these components.

Some (e.g., Crabtree et al., 2009) argue that the only purpose of an ethnographic study in HCI is to inform system design. Others (e.g., Dourish, 2006) argue that designers need a rich understanding of the situation for which they are designing, and that one of the important roles for ethnography is to expose and describe that context for design, without necessarily making the explicit link to implications for design. The best designs are usually ones where the design team has a rich understanding of the intended users of their products. We are often reminded of the power of intuitive design (e.g., Moggridge, 2007), but when the design team cannot have good intuitions about their users, they need other means to put themselves in the user's shoes. Rich qualitative studies describing people, technology and work have a valuable role to play in HCI: in particular, for the design and evaluation of technology, agenda setting, theory creation and critique of predominant design paradigms.

Figure 2.2: Planning and preparation is of paramount importance to ensure that decisions about direction, sampling, editing, etc., result in a coherent and achievable project.

## 2.2    PLANNING AND PREPARATION

One way to think about the planning of a study is in terms of the PRET A Rapporter (PRETAR) framework (Blandford et al., 2008a). This is a basic structure for designing, conducting and reporting studies:

- **P**urpose: every study has a purpose, which may be more or less precisely defined; methods should be selected to address the purpose of the study. The purpose of a study may change as understanding develops, but few people are able to conduct an effective study without some idea of why they are doing it.

- **R**esources and constraints: all studies must be conducted with the available resources, also taking account of existing constraints that may limit what is possible.

- **E**thical considerations often shape what is possible, particularly in terms of how data can be gathered and results reported.

- **T**echniques for data gathering need to be determined (working with the available resources to address the purpose of the study).

- **A**nalysis techniques need to be appropriate to the data and the purpose of the study.

- **R**eporting needs to address the purpose of the study, and communicate it effectively to the intended audiences. In some cases, this will include an account of how and why the purpose has evolved, as well as the methods, results, etc.

To tackle a project competently you will need to build up relevant expertise in qualitative research and in the study domain. There is no shortcut to acquiring that expertise. Courses, textbooks and research papers provide essential foundations, and different resources resonate with (and are therefore most useful to) different people. Corbin and Strauss (2015) emphasise the importance of planning and practice: "Persons sometimes think that they can go out into the field and conduct interviews or observations with no training or preparation. Often these persons are disappointed when the data they are able to gather are sparse" (p. 37). Kidder and Fine (1987) describe the evolving focus of qualitative research: that one of the researcher's frequent tasks is "deciding which question to ask next of whom" (p. 60). There is no substitute for planning, practice and reflecting on what can be learnt from each interview or observation session.

It is tempting to want to apply a precisely defined method (Yardley, 2000). But, in all probability, you will be faced by complexity that demands some improvisation along the way (Furniss et al., 2011a; Woolrych et al., 2011). We provide a series of checklists to help focus on particular decisions when designing, conducting and reporting a study.

As well as expertise in qualitative methods, the level of expertise in the study context can have a huge influence over the quality and kind of study conducted. When the study focuses on a widely used technology or an activity that most people engage in, such as time management (e.g., Kamsin et al., 2012) or in-car navigation (e.g., Curzon et al., 2002), any disparity in expertise between researcher and participants is unlikely to be critical. Where the study is of a highly specialised device, or in a specialist context, the expertise of the researcher(s) can have a significant effect on both the conduct and the outcomes of a study. At times, naiveté can be an asset, allowing one to ask simple but important questions that would be overlooked by someone with more domain expertise. At other times, naiveté can result in the researcher failing to note or interpret important features of the study context. In preparing to conduct a study, it is important to consider the effects of expertise and to determine whether or not specific training in the technology or work being studied is required before data-gathering starts.

Rather than trying to anticipate every possible eventuality, it is often best to do *enough* preparation, where what constitutes enough is likely to vary from one individual to another as well as from one study question to another. So, as a starting point, we summarise an idealised shape of a qualitative study (Figure 2.3): you start with a purpose (a research question), then you gather and analyse data, to yield results that are then reported (in a dissertation, paper or client report); the study is shaped by various factors, including the expertise of the research team (discussed above), resources and constraints, the role of theory and ethical considerations (all discussed below).

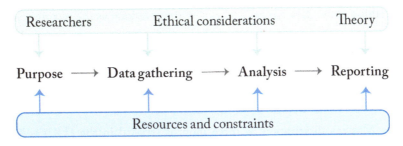

Figure 2.3: An idealised shape of a qualitative study.

Although we first present steps sequentially and simply, you should be aware that this is an over-simplification: it is hardly ever possible to separate the components of a study and treat them independently. The style of data gathering influences what analysis can be performed; the relationship established with early participants may influence the recruitment of later participants; ethical considerations may influence what kinds of data can be gathered, etc. Managing these interdependencies can make qualitative research particularly challenging at times, but successfully juggling and trading them off also makes qualitative research interesting and rewarding. We return to this topic of interdependencies later.

## 2.3    BEING REALISTIC: RESOURCES AND CONSTRAINTS

Every study has to be designed to work with the available resources. Where resources are limited it is necessary to "cut your coat according to your cloth." For example, if you have three months to conduct a Master's project you will need to fit ambitions, and hence purpose, to what is possible with the available resources. Here are some things to consider when thinking about the time involved for a qualitative study:

- **Time to obtain ethical clearance** will depend on how sensitive the study is and which review board is assessing it; you can often get local knowledge to help you plan this.

- **Time to recruit** participants also depends on their situations and how interesting the topic is to them. Recruiting through a general subject pool can often be quick, but if you are seeking participants with specialist skills or knowledge, you should factor in significant time for this.

- The mean **duration** of an interview is under an hour, depending on the scope of the interviews. Few interviews are much longer than that because attention drifts. Observations can be longer (several hours per session with comfort breaks).

- **Transcribing** audio data typically takes 4–6 times as long as the recording, depending on data quality, lengths of silences and the transcriber's typing speed. Transcribing video data takes significantly longer, depending on the level of detail being transcribed.

- **Analysis time** can vary, depending on the quality of the data and the depth and focus of analysis, but is likely to take at least 2–3 days per hour of data.

In total, a Master's dissertation of three months (typical in the U.K.) is likely to involve 10–15 hours of audio data, or equivalent. That does not sound like much, but is usually all that is feasible when all the other stages of the project (including literature review and writing up) are taken into account. It is therefore important that the data should be as high quality as possible.

As well as time, resource considerations need to cover funding, equipment available for data collection and analysis, availability of places to conduct the study, availability of participants and expertise. Here, we briefly discuss some of these issues, while avoiding stating the obvious (variants on the theme of "don't plan to use resources that you don't have or can't acquire!").

Where a study takes place can shape that study significantly. Studies that take place within the context of work, home or other natural setting are sometimes referred to as "situated" or "in the wild" (e.g., Rogers, 2012). Studies that take place in more controlled settings include laboratory studies (e.g., involving think-aloud protocol) and some interview studies. There are also intermediate points, such as the use of simulation labs, or the use of spaces that are similar to the work setting, where participants have access to some, but not all, features of the natural work setting. Observational studies most commonly take place "in the wild," where the "wild" may be a workplace, the home, or some other location where the technology of interest is used. Interview studies may take place in the "wild" or in another place that is comfortable for participants, and quiet enough to record and to ensure appropriate privacy and safety for both participant and interviewer. Of course, there are also study types where researcher and participant are at a distance from each other, such as diary studies and remote interviews.

Tools for data recording include notes, audio recording, still camera, video camera and screen capture software. All of these can be useful, depending on the situations and purpose for which data is being gathered.

**Hand-written or typed notes** can be most effective in noisy environments, or where there are sensitivities about any other form of recording. Care needs to be taken that the act of note-taking does not disrupt the interaction. For example, if particular actions are noted in an observation session, participants may be aware of every time a note is taken, and hence self-conscious about the activity that is provoking the note-taking (Blandford et al., 2015a).

**Audio recording** is often most suitable for interviews and focus groups. If you are working on your own it might be difficult to follow and facilitate the interview and note down all the important points otherwise. Audio recording and transcription is also needed where the details of specific words and phrases people use are important. Audio recordings are preferable to note-taking particularly when the study is exploratory and there is a chance that information that might be overlooked early on turns out to be important later, or if the data is rich enough to support multiple analyses. For example, Rajkomar et al. (2015) originally gathered data on people's situated use of home haemodialysis technology in order to test and extend the DiCoT approach (Furniss and Blandford, 2006) to analysing a system in terms of Distributed Cognition (DCog: Hollan et al., 2000). Within the initial interview plan, we intentionally also addressed questions of basic usability and how people stay safe on home haemodialysis (Rajkomar et al., 2014). Another unanticipated theme within the data was how people cope with managing their own dialysis at home including, but not limited to, how they troubleshoot when the technology goes wrong (Blandford et al., 2015b). It would not have been possible for us to do this follow-up Thematic Analysis without full audio transcriptions of the interviews.

**Still photographs** of activities performed and equipment/technology used provide a permanent record to support analysis and for illustrative purposes in reports. This can be particularly useful when the equipment has been adapted by users, or for recording where technology was used or how it was configured. For example, Figure 2.4 shows a series of photos of glucometers used in a hospital that supported analysis of the system in terms of DCog (Furniss et al., 2015).

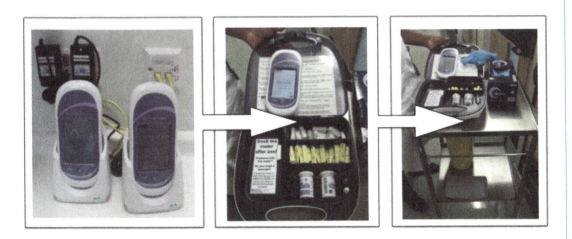

Figure 2.4: Glucometer use in a hospital. The same device is shown stand-alone (left), as part of a blood glucose testing kit (middle) and as part of a broader blood glucose testing system (right).

**Video recording** can be valuable for capturing the details of an interaction, but can be intrusive. Recording video can be particularly useful for capturing micro-interactions and interaction that involves the use of equipment or technology in a particular physical space (e.g., in a family car—see Cycil et al., 2014) or involves multiple users interacting with technology (see Marshall et al., 2011).

**Screen capture software** can give a valuable record of user interactions with desktop systems. For capturing rarely performed interactions, or interactions over an extended time period (e.g., how a document is written over a period of days or weeks), it may be possible to ask participants to record their own screens or to take screenshots (e.g., Karlson et al., 2010).

Particular qualitative methods may require specialist equipment for data gathering. Examples include the use of cultural probes (Gaver and Dunne, 1999), which involve participants receiving a set of tools such as cameras, notebooks, pens and sticky notes with which to record their experiences, or engaging participants in keeping video diaries. Other specialist tools may sometimes add value; for example, eye gaze tracking, motion capture or activity tracking may add useful quantitative data to complement the qualitative in some studies (see discussion of mixed methods in Chapter 6).

When it comes to data analysis, colored pencils, highlighter pens and paper are often adequate for studies that involve only a few hours of data. For larger studies, computer-based Qualitative Data Analysis tools (e.g., NVivo, MaxQDA, Dedoose or ATLAS.ti) can help with managing and keeping track of data, but require time to learn to use effectively. These tools can help track large quantities of quotations, codes, links and memos. They can also speed up the process of analysis; for example, they allow you to rapidly change the name of every instance of a particular code, or list every quotation with a particular code. However, they do not actually do any of the sense making themselves—that is left to the researcher.

As well as the costs of equipment, the other main costs for studies are typically the costs of travel and participant fees. Within HCI, there has been little discussion around the ethics and practicality of paying participant fees for studies. In disciplines where this has been studied (most notably medicine), there is little agreement on policy for paying participants (e.g., Grady et al., 2005; Fry et al., 2005). The ethical concerns in medicine are typically much greater than those in HCI due to the level of potential harm. In HCI, it is common practice to recompense participants for their time and any costs they incur, with cash or gift certificates, without making the payment so large that people are likely to participate just for the money.

Often, the biggest constraint is access to a study setting or availability of suitable participants; we devote the next chapter to this topic.

## 2.4    ETHICS AND INFORMED CONSENT

Traditionally, ethics has been concerned with the avoidance of harm, and most established ethical clearance processes focus on this. "VIP" is a useful mnemonic for the main considerations:

- Vulnerable participants

- **I**nformed consent

- **P**rivacy and confidentiality

Particular care needs to be taken when recruiting participants from groups that might be regarded as vulnerable, such as children, the elderly or people with a particular condition (illness, addiction, etc.).

In providing informed consent, participants should be told the purpose of the study, and made aware of their right to withdraw at any time without reason and without them being at any disadvantage. If it is not possible to inform participants of the full purpose of the study at the outset (e.g., because this might bias their behaviour and defeat the object of the study), then they should be debriefed fully at the end of the study.

It is common practice to provide a written information sheet outlining the purpose of the study, what is expected of participants, how their data will be stored, used and, if applicable, shared and how findings will be reported. Depending on the circumstances, it may be appropriate to gather either written or verbal consent; if written then the record should be kept securely, and separately from data. Preece et al. (2015) suggest that requiring participants to sign an informed consent form helps to keep the relationship between researcher and participants "clear and professional." This is true in some situations, but not in others, where verbal consent may be less disruptive for participants. For example, verbal consent may work better if observing someone briefly while they go about their work, if getting written consent would disrupt the work disproportionately.

With the growing use of social media, and of research methods making use of such data (e.g., from Twitter or online forums), there are situations where gathering informed consent is impractical or maybe even impossible. In such situations, it is important to weigh up the value of the research and how to ensure that confidentiality and respect are maintained. Bear in mind that although such data has been made publicly available, the authors may not have considered all possible uses of the data and may feel a strong sense of ownership of it. If in doubt, discuss possible ethical concerns with experts in research ethics.

Privacy and confidentiality should be respected in data gathering, management and reporting. Some of this is covered in data protection laws and information governance procedures. It is good practice to anonymise data as soon as is practical, i.e., when taking notes or transcribing audio. This means replacing people's names with a participant number (e.g., "P3") or pseudonym, and removing other proper nouns that have the potential to personally identify participants (e.g., company names, specific places, such as the name of a small town, etc.). It may be necessary to retain contact details securely so that it is possible to inform participants of the outcome of the study later, but this would normally only be done with informed consent, for participants who want to know more.

Ethics goes beyond the principle of no harm: it should also be about doing good. There must be some value in the research, otherwise it is not worth doing. This might require a long-term perspective: understanding current design and user experiences to guide the design of future technologies. That long-term view may not give research participants immediate pay-back, but where possible there should be benefits to participating in a study. In our experience, participants have responded positively to us explaining that findings from their study will not be used to inform the design of the technology they actually use, but with the aim of making this sort of technology easier to use for people in the future.

It is important to review the safety of the researcher as well as that of participants. This commonly involves doing a risk analysis. For example, researchers should meet participants who are not already known to them in public spaces wherever possible. For home studies, it is generally good practice to work in pairs, or to consider other ways of mitigating any risks.

## 2.5    ACCOMMODATING RESEARCHER BIASES AND PRE-EXISTING THEORY WHEN PLANNING A STUDY

In addition to resources, constraints and ethical considerations, there are various less tangible factors that shape any study. Probably the most important are the ways that pre-existing theory can be used to inform data gathering, analysis and reporting of a study, and also the biases, understanding, and experience of the researcher(s) involved in the project (Denzin and Lincoln, 2011).

No researcher is a *tabula rasa*: each comes to a study with pre-existing understanding, experience, interests, etc. Hertzum and Jacobsen (2001) studied how several analysts independently identified usability difficulties from the same video data in which other participants had been thinking aloud while interacting with a user interface. There was significant variability in what issues their participating analysts identified. They considered this to be "chilling": that there is no objective, shared understanding, even with an activity as superficially simple as identifying usability difficulties from think-aloud data. If this is true for analysing pre-determined data with a pre-defined question, it clearly has an even greater effect when the researcher is shaping the entire study.

For the individual, it may be difficult to identify or articulate many of the factors that shape the research they conduct, but one obvious factor is the role of theory in a study. Theory may shape the research from the outset, come into play during the analysis, or be most prominent towards the end of a research project. In Chapter 6, we discuss how theory may be introduced in an analysis, and how it can contribute to the generalisability of findings. Here, we focus on how it may be used to shape a study at the planning stage.

Theory may be introduced early into a study: either to test an existing theory in a new context or to better understand the study context while having a focus that helps to manage its complexity. A theory can act as a "lens," providing sensitising concepts that help to shape and focus data gathering and impose a partial structure on the data that is gathered. Similarly, a theory can help in shaping analysis.

Where this is done, it is important not to trust an existing theoretical framework unquestioningly, but to test and extend that framework: are there counter-examples that challenge the accuracy of the existing framework? Are there examples that go beyond the framework and introduce important extensions to it? Many studies that introduce theory early end up extending or refining the theory and also making the study more manageable. For example, when studying the interactive behaviour of lawyers when looking for information on the Web (Makri et al., 2008a), we shaped our approach to data gathering and analysis around the work of Ellis et al. (1993) and Ellis and Haugan (1997). While this was not our intention at the beginning of the study, as our study evolved we noticed that many of the interactive behaviours the lawyers displayed were highly similar to those identified by Ellis and colleagues in other disciplines (and when using electronic library catalogues rather than the Web). Later data gathering and analysis focused on Ellis's model. However, rather than assume that all of Ellis and colleagues' findings applied in this new context, we questioned their total fit. This resulted in the existing theory being enriched by both extending and refining previous findings. A different example of contributing to theory arose from our attempts to apply DCog to analyse a control room. DCog is a theoretical perspective that views cognition as being distributed in the world, rather than residing solely in the mind, recognising the role of artefacts and information flow in supporting cognition. We found the theory lacked a suitable method to apply it, so we developed a method called DiCoT (Distributed Cognition for Teamwork) to fill this gap (Furniss and Blandford, 2006). Sometimes contributions to theory and method can be greater than the insights for the context under study.

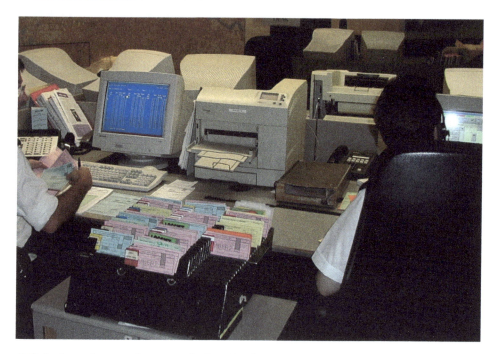

Figure 2.5: A view of a control room with shared information artefacts that shaped the development of DiCoT (Furniss and Blandford, 2006).

## 2.6    SUMMARY AND CHECKLIST: PLANNING A STUDY

Just as the director of a documentary film is driven by their vision and has to plan what and where to film within their constraints before starting, you have to think about your study's purpose and plan before you start to gather data. You might review relevant literature and do a pilot study early on to check your study design or to shape your approach. You might consult with a specialist user group to check your plans are feasible. You might need to review the focus of your study or approach as a result. But without a plan, a study is unlikely to be robust or deliver useful outcomes. There comes a point when you simply have to head off and explore, because if you knew ahead of time what you were going to find in the study, there would be no point in doing it. But it is wise to know broadly what you want to study and how before you begin. It is also wise to write up the study method ahead of time, to capture what you propose to do; this "methods" section can be reviewed and revised later if you discover that what you had intended was not in practice feasible or appropriate.

Checklist A summarises issues that need to be considered early on. You should also be mindful of quality considerations (discussed in Chapter 8) from the outset, to make sure that you conduct and report the best possible study.

| Checklist A: Planning a SSQS | |
|---|---|
| **Purpose** | What is the purpose of the study? Why is it an important study to conduct? What gap in knowledge is it filling? |
| **Resources and constraints** | What resources do you have to work with? What constraints limit possibilities? What training and preparation does each researcher need? What expertise does the researcher bring to the project? Do you need advocate(s) within the study setting? How will you identify and work with them? See Chapter 3. What is the approach to sampling participants? How will participants be recruited? See Chapter 3. Where will the study take place? To what extent, and how, will theory play a role in data gathering, analysis and/or reporting? |
| **Ethical considerations** | Are there important ethical considerations that need to be addressed (e.g., vulnerable participants)? How will you ensure that participants benefit as far as possible from participation? What will participants be told about the study when giving informed consent? How will participants be debriefed about the study once it is completed? How will data be stored and anonymised? How will participants' engagement be reported? If participants read the report, will they feel well represented or is there a risk that they might feel used or misled? See Chapter 7. Have you considered your own safety and health and made sure that this is addressed well (e.g., considering the risks of lone working)? |
| **Techniques for data gathering** | How will data be gathered (interviews, observation, etc.)? How will it be recorded? If multiple methods are to be used, how will they be sequenced and co-ordinated? How interleaved will participant recruitment, data gathering and analysis be? |
| **Analysis of data** | How will data be analysed? How will the analysis be validated or will quality be ensured/assessed? |
| **Reporting** | Who is the audience? How will findings be reported? |

# CHAPTER 3

# Sampling and Recruitment

## WHO AND WHAT TO FILM?

In creating a documentary, the director and editor can only work with the footage they have, so it is important for the filmmaker to choose good locations and camera angles, be patient, be creative and be lucky. Similarly, a key determinant of study outcome is the quality of the data that is gathered. As noted in the previous chapter, researcher factors (their expertise in qualitative research, in the domain or technology being studied and of any relevant theory) contribute to data quality. Other important determinants are the suitability of participants providing the data for the study, and often the rapport and trust that is built up between researcher and participant. In this chapter, we focus on strategies and challenges for recruiting participants.

An early question is likely to be where the study is to take place, or where participants are to be sourced from. There are four main places where studies are likely to be conducted: work places, participants' homes, public places chosen by the researcher (e.g., cafes) and laboratories and meeting rooms accessible to the researcher.

## 3.1 APPROACHES TO SAMPLING

When a study is conducted within an organisation, individual participants are most commonly recruited by an intermediary (or advocate) within the organisation, and you will need to be guided by them as to who are suitable participants. You may have ideas about the ideal profiles of participants; for example, people in particular roles or people with different attitudes to the technology in question. However, you will also need to work with people's availability, willingness to participate and what is possible within pragmatic constraints.

If the study is not linked to a particular organisation, you are usually directly responsible for (and in control of) recruitment.

When talking about recruitment of participants, most papers discuss this in terms of a sampling strategy. This is a strategic question: what kinds of people do you want as participants in your study? There is then the tactical question of how to recruit those participants.

Figure 3.1: What you choose to sample as well as the quality of the footage will have a direct impact on the quality and outcome of the project.

Sampling criteria are often quite broad (e.g., people who enjoy playing video games) and then it is possible to recruit through public advertising. Sometimes, they are focused (e.g., people with a particular job role using a specific technology within an organisation). For other studies, the aim might be to obtain a representative sample; for example, in a study of lawyers' use of digital information tools (Makri et al., 2008a), our aim was to involve lawyers across the range of seniority, from undergraduate students to partners in a law firm and professors in a university law department. This allowed us to observe how a wide variety of lawyers used existing tools. An alternative approach might have been to observe lawyers from a representative sample of different legal specialisms.

Miles and Huberman (1994, p. 28) list no fewer than 16 different approaches to sampling, such as maximum variation, extreme or deviant case, typical case and stratified purposeful, each with a particular value in terms of data gathering and analysis. The kind of probability sampling that is commonly reported in quantitative studies, where the aim is to sample participants to maximise the likelihood of them being representative of the total population, is rarely appropriate or even possible in qualitative studies. Common sampling strategies reported in qualitative HCI studies are:

1. **Purposive sampling** (also called **judgment sampling**): This involves selecting a sample of participants who are most likely to address the research question efficiently. The study of lawyers outlined above followed this approach. Segerståhl and Oinas-Kukkonen (2011) describe an approach they call "purposive intensity sampling" that aimed to recruit participants who were likely to use the product of interest (for monitoring exercise) based on several inclusion and exclusion criteria.

2. **Theoretical sampling:** This is advocated within GT, and involves recruiting participants who are most likely to test, expand and help build the theory that is emerging through data gathering and analysis. This approach is only possible when data collection and analysis are interleaved and a theory is gradually developed through a cyclic process (see Chapter 6). Pace (2004) gives a clear account of an approach to studying the flow experience of people using the Web.

3. **Convenience sampling:** This involves working with the most accessible participants, and is therefore the easiest approach. Few papers explicitly report using a convenience sample, but research that involves other academics, such as Pontis et al. (2015), are often taking advantange of the comparative ease of recruiting from this population.

4. **Snowball sampling:** Each participant introduces the researcher to further participants who satisfy their inclusion criteria. This can be particularly useful for accessing hard-to-reach populations (e.g., people using a particular specialist device), but risks limiting participant diversity and consequent generalisability of findings. Makri et al. (2014) used snowball sampling to gain access to creative professionals: a composer knew a choreographer who knew a comedian and we were able to leverage these existing contacts to grow our sample.

Slightly tongue-in-cheek, Atkinson and Flint (2001) discuss "scrounging sampling": the increasingly desperate acquisition of participants to make up numbers almost regardless of suitability. While few authors admit to applying scrounging sampling as a strategy for recruitment, it may be better than nothing when all other strategies have failed. Whatever sampling strategy is adopted, the devil is in the details: in how participants have been recruited and the likely consequences of the recruitment strategy on what data is gathered and hence what the findings are. It is also possible to mix sampling approaches. For example, it is possible to adopt a purposive sampling approach at first then to use theoretical sampling if early findings suggest that new insights might be gained from additional or alternative types of participants. It is also possible to start with convenience sampling and snowball your way to more participants.

## 3.2   SAMPLING IN PRACTICE: RECRUITING PARTICIPANTS

The choice of recruitment methods depends on the purpose of the study, the sampling strategy and the kinds of participants needed. Possible approaches include:

- **Direct contact:** approaching individuals in the workplace (with authorisation from local managers if needed), or approaching people in public spaces (with due regard for safety, informed consent, etc.).

- **Indirect contact:** through advertising on noticeboards in physical spaces, through targeted email lists, via online lists and social media.

- **Mediated contact:** an introduction by someone else, such as a line manager in the workplace, another "gatekeeper" (e.g., teacher, or the organiser of a relevant special interest group), friends or other participants, as with snowball sampling.

As social media and other technologies evolve, new approaches to recruiting study participants are emerging. What matters is that the approach to recruitment is effective in terms of recruiting both a suitable number of participants and appropriate participants for the aims of the study. Different ethical considerations are important for different recruitment approaches; for example, potential participants should not perceive direct contact as aggressive or intrusive.

When recruiting participants for a study, with or without the advocacy of an intermediary, it is important to consider their motivations for participating. This is partly coupled with ethical considerations, and partly with how to incentivise people to participate at all. People may agree or elect to participate in studies for many different reasons. If you are a student, people may be willing to help with your study because they value education.

People may just want to be helpful if participating is low-cost in terms of time and effort. This was probably the case in our studies of ambulance control (e.g., Blandford and Wong, 2004), where we sat alongside controllers as they worked, and asked them about their work and their experience of their dispatch system in slack periods when they were waiting for the next call. In this case, the immediate benefits to participants were small, beyond the sense that someone else was interested in their work and valued their expertise. However, the cost of participation was also low.

In other cases, participants may be inherently interested in the research, as in some of our work on serendipity (Makri and Blandford, 2012) where several participants mentioned they agreed to take part because they thought serendipity was a "cool" concept. If the study involves using a novel technology, there may also be elements of curiosity, and opportunities to learn and have fun. They might also perceive some personal benefit. For example, participants in our studies on time management benefited from the chance to reflect on how they managed their time (Kamsin et al., 2012). Some people may participate for financial reward, or to return a favor.

Corbin and Strauss (2015) suggest that one reason for participating in a study may be making one's voice heard. Be aware that people may have their own agenda to promote, e.g., to complain about staff shortages or promote an issue they believe in. There may be forms of self-promotion where people want to be associated with what they say. Anonymising what people say can reduce the biases this might introduce on the data, as they will neither benefit nor be damaged by what is reported. There may also be forms of self-preservation where people feel threatened by being associated with what they say. For example, in one study of medical technologies (Rajkomar et al., 2014), participants were concerned that admitting to difficulties with the use of a technology could reflect poorly on their competence rather than the usability of the equipment. It is important to make it clear to participants that it is the interactive system, not them, that is under scrutiny and that taking part in the research will not disadvantage them in any way. This should be in deeds as well as words. Adopting a humble, relaxed approach to interviews and observations can make participants feel at ease. Explaining the purpose of the study to participants at the outset can reassure them that it really is the system and not them that is being tested. This is a positive aspect of properly informed consent; however, doubts might still remain. In our study of medical technologies, this approach was not enough. If we had known about participants' fears of their rights to use the equipment being revoked when planning the study, we would have emphasised that the usability issues they flagged would *only* be used to improve the design of the equipment, would not be disclosed to others (e.g., management) and would not be used to make decisions about rights to use the equipment.

There are many other complex motivations for participating in particular research projects. As researchers, we need to better understand those motivations, respect them and work with them.

One issue to remain aware of is bias in recruitment, although it is often impossible to avoid completely. Particularly when taking a convenience sample, such as recruiting friends-of-friends or people who have signed up to a subject pool, there is a high chance that the participant population is not representative of the broader population of people who might use the technology of interest. Also, people with particular motivations, such as particularly negative or positive prior experiences, may sign up readily to a study. Conversely, those who have less personal motivation to participate are more difficult to recruit; for example, some people may be concerned that their competence will be questioned. As well as this kind of "consent bias," there may also be "gatekeeper bias" in mediated contact, where those in authority (e.g., clinicians or teachers) filter out potential participants who they consider less suitable. In mediated contact there may also be "brownie point bias," where participants who have little personal motivation to participate do so because they want to please someone in authority such as their boss. This is only likely to cause problems if the participant's lack of motivation results in poor data. These biases will limit the generalisability of findings—a theme to which we return in Chapter 8.

## 3.3    SAMPLING IN PRACTICE: NEGOTIATING ACCESS

Studies in organisational workplaces can be both the easiest and the most difficult to organise. Easy because if individuals are participating as part of their ongoing work then identifying and working with those individuals is usually fairly straightforward, provided that local managers are supportive. But there can be a significant up-front investment in negotiating access to the study site unless the site has some prior interest or engagement in the study.

Where studies are devised and run in collaboration with problem owners (e.g., Randell et al., 2013), negotiating access is generally straightforward. Where this is not the case, it is essential to identify promising study sites and individuals who will act as advocates for the study. For example, given the shift in emphasis in healthcare from hospital to home, we are interested in how medical devices are taken up and used in the home, and how products that were originally developed for use by clinical staff in hospitals can be adapted for home use. There are some products that are well established for home use, such as nebulisers and blood glucose monitors, and others that are making the transition from hospital to home, such as patient-controlled analgesia and intravenous administration of chemotherapy. We followed several lines of enquiry to identify clinicians who expressed an interest in patients' experiences of intravenous therapies at home, but all eventually drew a blank. In contrast, we identified several renal clinicians who were sufficiently interested in patients' experience of home haemodialysis to introduce us to their patients. This led to a productive study (Rajkomar et al., 2014; 2015) in which we identified not just the importance of the technology design, but also the importance of the social structures around technology use that impact the quality of patient care (Figure 3.2).

In all cases, it is important to consider why the study is valuable, what the costs and benefits to the organisation are, and why the organisation would want to participate. Ultimately though, it is about engaging with, and persuading, individuals within the organisation that the project is worth supporting and facilitating. There may be an initial cost in negotiating support from advocates, but this often brings with it the benefits of close engagement with the study domain, introductions to potential participants and longer-term impact through the engagement of stakeholders. Engaging with advocates at the planning stage, rather than just the recruitment stage, can improve buy-in by getting their input into the focus and design of the study early on.

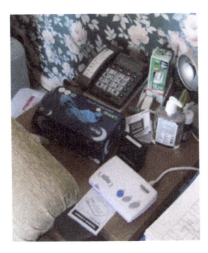

Figure 3.2: Communication devices in a home care setting. With the support of healthcare professionals as advocates, we found that not just technology design, but also the social structures around technology use impact the quality of patient care.

## 3.4    HOW MANY PARTICIPANTS?

A common question is: how many participants are needed for a qualitative study? Or, in the case of a situated observational study, how many hours of observation are needed? There are several possible answers to these questions:

- **The theory-based answer:** If you are following an approach such as GT, where data gathering and analysis are interleaved and theory is being constructed, then data gathering and analysis should continue until "theoretical saturation" is achieved. This is the point where gathering and analysing more data on the chosen theme does not yield further insight. The number of participants (or hours of data gathering) required to reach theoretical saturation will depend on the richness of the theory and of the data.

- **The moderately pragmatic answer:** the largest dataset that can be meaningfully handled to yield reliable insights. Perhaps surprisingly, for a Ph.D. this is rarely more than 30–40 hours of rich qualitative data.

- **The very pragmatic answer:** you gather as much data as it is possible to gather and analyse well in the time available. The "sweet spot" between quantity of data and quality of analysis depends on the richness of the data. As noted above, for a 3-month MSc project, it is difficult to gather and analyse more than 10–15 hours of interview data.

Time is often an important factor: it can take a long time to recruit each participant, arrange and conduct data gathering, transcribe and analyse the data. Another factor might be the availability of participants who satisfy the recruitment criteria (e.g., people who hold a particular role in an organisation or have particular experience). A shorter study with fewer participants needs to be more focused, because otherwise it risks delivering shallow data from which it is almost impossible to derive valuable insight.

A typical structure for a GT study (see Chapter 6) might be to interview and analyse data from 3–4 participants to begin to familiarise yourself with the data. You could then continue to explore themes and patterns up to about 12 participants, perhaps reaching theoretical saturation. For larger projects, such as some Ph.D. research, you may expand the scope of the developing theory, using the principle of theoretical sampling to engage selectively with a different group of participants.

Although not common in HCI, it is possible to conduct a study with a single participant, as a rich case study. For example, Attfield et al. (2008) gathered observations, interview data and examples of artefacts produced from a single journalist as that journalist prepared an article from inception to publication. The aim of the study was to understand the phases of work, how information was transformed through that work and how technology supported the work. Such a case study provides a rich understanding of the interaction, but care has to be taken with generalising from this. Ideally, such a case needs to be compared with known features of comparable cases, in terms of both similarities and contrasts. In poorly understood areas, even a single rich case study can add to our overall understanding of the design, deployment and use of interactive technologies. But most qualitative HCI studies involve at least ten participants.

It would be great to have more reliable ways of planning numbers of participants. In quantitative research, there are tools to help calculate the power of a study, from which it is possible to calculate how many participants are needed to achieve statistical significance if the hypothesised relation between dependent and independent variables holds. Fugard and Potts (2015) have tried to extend this style of reasoning to qualitative studies; however, they are forced to make so many simplifying assumptions about the nature of the study and of the data that there are very few situations in which their tool might be reliably applied for exploratory studies. In particular, it is generally difficult to anticipate what themes will be of interest when planning an exploratory study, and how those themes will relate to each other.

In summary, there are qualitative approaches where it is useful to plan the number of participants ahead of time, but for most semi-structured qualitative studies this can only be done very roughly and it will have two main drivers to choosing the number of participants: theoretical aims and pragmatic constraints, as discussed above.

# 3.5    SUMMARY AND CHECKLIST: RECRUITING PARTICIPANTS

Like the director and filmmaker, you have to decide where to gather data and from whom. You should do your best to create the conditions in which the data that is gathered is likely to be of high quality. When planning a study, it is important to consider recruitment and relationship management. Throughout, it is important to remain aware of participants' motivations for participating, and the potential benefits and disadvantages they might perceive from doing so. When dealing with sensitive topics where people may have reasons for sharing or withholding certain information, or for behaving in particular ways, it is also important to be aware of motivations and their possible effects on the data that is gathered. It is particularly important in these cases to review your data gathering techniques to maximise the likelihood of gathering valid data and to reflect on the quality of your data and the implications for your findings.

Checklist B summarises considerations relating to recruitment.

| Checklist B: Recruiting participants | |
|---|---|
| **Resources and constraints** | What is the approach to sampling participants? What are inclusion and exclusion criteria? |
| | Where will the study take place? |
| | Are advocate(s) within the study setting required? How will they be identified and engaged? |
| | How will participants be recruited? |
| | Where and when to work with participants during the process of data gathering, and how (or whether) to engage with them more broadly from the start to the end of a study. |
| **Ethical considerations** | Are there important ethical considerations that need to be addressed (e.g., vulnerable participants)? |
| | How will participants benefit from participation? |
| | What will participants be told about the study when giving informed consent? |
| | How will participants be reassured their data will be treated confidentially? |
| | How will participants be debriefed about the study once it is completed? |

# CHAPTER 4

# Gathering Data

### *GETTING FOOTAGE*

Once overall decisions about the focus of the documentary and the locations for filming have been made, it is time for the film crew to gather footage. As anyone who has watched behind-the-scenes accounts from wildlife documentaries will know, the gathering of footage requires a variety of techniques, from filming sequences with the narrator on location to using powerful long lenses or specialist cameras, e.g., for underwater shots. Sometimes things do not go according to plan, such as when the subject of the documentary fails to show up or attacks the camera, and rapid re-planning is needed. Conversely, at other times, unanticipated, delightful things may happen, such as capturing a very rare behaviour or interaction between animals. The same can be true of qualitative data gathering: it may be valuable to apply complementary techniques to obtain richer data that yields deeper insight. There will be moments of surprise and delight, but there will also be times of frustration and challenge, when things do not go according to plan and there is a need to improvise or change direction.

The analyst can only work with the data that is collected. Therefore, it is important to gather the best possible data, working within the resources of the project. The most common techniques for gathering data are discussed below: observation, semi-structured interviews, think-aloud, focus groups and diary studies. The increasing focus on the use of technologies while mobile, in the home, and in other locations are leading to yet more ways of gathering qualitative data. As Rode (2011, p.123) notes: "as new technologies develop, they allow new possibilities for fieldwork—remote interviews, participant-observation through games, or blogs, or virtual worlds, and following the lives of one's informants via Twitter." The possibilities are seemingly endless, and growing. The limit may be the imagination of the research team. We have chosen to focus on established techniques because they are the most widely used, and because many of the same basic skills are required for more novel methods exploiting new technologies.

Whatever method(s) of data collection are employed, it is wise to pilot test them before launching into extensive data gathering. This is to check that the data gathering is as effective as possible and to ensure that the resulting data can be analysed as planned to address the purpose of the study. If the study design is highly iterative then it is important to review the approach to data gathering before every data gathering episode, e.g., as described using GT (Chapter 6).

## 4.1    THE ROLE OF THE RESEARCHER

Before presenting an overview of methods for gathering data, we will briefly review the roles of the researcher, in particular, their relationship with participants. Are they more like a "fly on the wall" that does not impact the participant or situation, or are they more like an active participant in the situation that does influence the context?

Some kinds of studies, such as diary studies and think-aloud studies, typically involve little engagement between the researcher and participant. Once these types of studies are initiated the researcher is reliant on having designed it well and on participants providing data as anticipated. Good pilot testing is advised! Such studies are relatively easy to describe in terms of how participants were instructed. Interventions by the researcher may be planned, and may nudge data gathering. However, on the whole, the approach does not evolve significantly during the study, and the role of the researcher is limited. For example, it is likely that substituting one researcher for another would have little effect on what data is gathered. Arguably, the same is true of relatively structured interview and observational studies. However, it is important to be aware of, and reflect on, the potential effect that data gathering may have on participants' behaviour.

In many documentaries it is apparent that the subjects' behaviour is influenced by the presence of the camera. Similarly, many subscribe to the view that it is not possible to conduct a study of a situation without both influencing and being influenced by that situation. Being observed influences participants' behaviour. The researcher's challenge is to limit the influence of data gathering on the data that is gathered. Like "fly on the wall" documentaries, some observational studies involve the researcher trying to minimise the effect of their presence on the activity being observed by avoiding asking questions. Then, for some studies, it may be a reasonable approximation to assume that the presence of the researcher has little influence on the data that is gathered. However, it is important to reflect on the likelihood that observational factors such as the Hawthorne effect, in which participants were found to perform better when being observed (Roethlisberger and Dickson, 1939), might have an impact on findings.

In interviews, the influence of the researcher is likely to be smallest when the interview is structured. While it is arguably impossible (perhaps even undesirable) to remove all traces of researcher influence from a study, it is possible to approach a piece of research with the intention to remain as open and unbiased as possible in order to minimise the influence of the researcher. For example, if the purpose of the study is to understand how a particular group of professionals use technology to support their working practices and the implications for design, the researcher may decide to observe the use of a broad range of technologies rather than restrict participants to using particular technologies. They might decide to observe with minimal intervention rather than ask questions. For example, in our study of how ambulance controllers use technology to maintain awareness of the situation, both within the control room and in the outside world of ambulances and incidents (Blandford and Wong, 2004), it seemed reasonable to assume that the way we related with study participants had little influence on their performance as professionals.

More active participation brings the researcher into the frame, and increases their influence on the data being gathered. This is most obvious in studies involving action research, in which the researcher is intentionally intervening and working with participants to assess the effects of interventions on perceptions, processes, and outcomes (Kock, 2013). It is also likely to be the case where the researcher acts as a participant observer, playing an active role within the study context, and to a lesser extent in approaches such as Contextual Inquiry (Holtzblatt and Beyer, 2013), which bring the researcher into the observation/interview space, though data gathering is still shaped mainly by the activities being performed (see Chapter 6). In our think-aloud observations of how professionals interact with information (Makri et al., 2008a; Makri and Warwick, 2010) we took a more active role than is usual in think-aloud studies. Here, we not only wanted to understand what professionals did when interacting with information, but also why they did what they did. We asked probing, opportunistic questions such as "what did you just do?" and "why did you click there?" While we cannot be certain that this did not influence participants' behaviour, we did not find any evidence of influence, e.g., changes in behaviour as a result of our questioning.

In some studies, the researcher and their relationship with participants is central to the research process. This relationship can have a strong influence on what information is shared with participants, how it is shared by participants, how it is interpreted by the researcher, and how it is reported. For example, Rode et al. (2004) discuss their approach of exploring families' use of programmable technologies in the home by using fuzzy felt props as being "provocative," aiming to establish "rich dialog" with participants. They describe the props as being effective mediating representations to support the conversation about programmable devices in the home to give a rich contextual understanding of use.

Semi-structured interviews inevitably bring in the interests of the researcher as well as the participant. To pretend that they are purely objective is to downplay the individuality of each researcher and the relationship between researcher and participant. The interview is a dialogue between people. Where the interview strays into potentially sensitive areas, such as negative feelings around technology use, it may even be unethical to remain artificially detached from the setting. In such situations, it is impossible to substitute one researcher for another without further changes. The researcher is shaping the conversation and the data that is gathered, and the extent of that shaping should be recognised and reported transparently and unapologetically.

Where the topic is one that participants might be sensitive about, it can sometimes help to have pre-existing common ground between the researcher doing data gathering and the participant, e.g., being of the same sex or a similar age. An example might be intimate health issues that are important for the design of some health behaviour change technologies and interactive medical devices. Where multiple researchers are available, this might mean matching them well to participants. Where there is a single researcher, it might mean reviewing the purpose of the study to be sure that data gathering is likely to be productive.

While the researcher may be an expert in HCI (or similar), it is the participants who are experts in their work and in living their lives; they may not always understand the details of the technologies that they use, but they have the greater understanding of their own situations and their needs. This differential expertise is at the heart of qualitative HCI studies. We normally recommend taking an apprentice stance during fieldwork (Beyer and Holtzblatt, 1998) but we have experienced situations where this has not felt appropriate. For example, while doing observational work on a ward we heard a complaint by a doctor that a device's alarm could neither be silenced nor turned down. The nurse said she had tried everything to turn the volume down but it did not work. Curious as to what the problem was and dissatisfied with the response because of the effect on the patient who was critically ill, we decided to help rather than just observe. The device's volume button alone only operated the pulse volume, while holding down the alarm silence button for three seconds and then using the volume controls operated the alarm volume, which the nurse did not know. We had to be sensitive in how we raised this issue with the nurse, as our expertise in interaction design challenged her position (Furniss, 2014).

It is also important to remember that participants may have an interest in the research and its outcomes after their participation in a study. In the short term, it may be important to manage their expectations where those expectations are unrealistic, e.g., of having a fully functioning new system within a few months. In the longer term, it is a courtesy to offer to keep participants and others who facilitate research informed of the outcomes of the research, though not all will want this.

In the following sections, we summarise the most common approaches to gathering data in qualitative HCI studies.

## 4.2   OBSERVATION

Put simply, observation involves watching and noting what happens, and usually takes place in the situation where the technology of interest is or will be used. The focus may be on work or leisure activities, and how the technology supports, hinders or otherwise shapes them, or on people's interactions with the technology. Observation is often complemented by interviews, e.g., Contextual Inquiry, described in Chapter 6. There are many possible forms of observation, and many dimensions on which observational studies may vary, including:

- The **extent to which participants are aware they are being observed**. Covert observation is unusual in HCI, but there are exceptions. In interaction labs there is often a one-way mirror to allow observation of participants. Participants are usually told they are being observed but they cannot see who is behind the mirror. Covert observation and one-way mirrors are also used in simulation labs, e.g., mock-up hospital operating theatres or home spaces.

- The **extent to which obtaining informed consent is necessary** for the observation. In some situations, it may not be feasible to seek infomed consent, such as when observing group interaction behaviour in public spaces. But it is still possible to let people know you are observing them by putting up signs, giving out leaflets, etc. If some people do not want to take part, you should delete any data that includes them. It is also essential to get permission from the owner of the space to conduct the observation.

- The **extent to which the observer becomes a participant** in the situation being observed. As discussed above, sometimes observers try to be unobtrusive; at other times they are clearly present in the situation. In action research (Chapter 6), where the researcher is intervening and assessing the effects of the intervention, the researcher is a key participant. In other situations, the researcher may minimise their active engagement, particularly if they are studying expert work in a domain which they have limited knowledge of.

- How **realistic the environment** in which observation takes place is. While many observational studies take place in the workplace, some take place in specially designed simulation laboratories (e.g., where there might be safety implications of working in the real environment), in specially instrumented "smart homes" (e.g., when studying how people interact with novel home technologies) or in laboratory settings (e.g., when studying people's interactions with a novel computer interface).

- Whether the observation is of **established systems** to support requirements gathering and understanding people's needs for **new systems**, or whether it involves an intervention such as the introduction of a novel technology. When new technology is introduced, the ways that people interact with that technology, or the way it changes their behaviour, is likely to be the focus of the observation.

- How **structured the observation notes** are. For some studies, where the objects of interest are clearly defined, observation notes may be highly structured and systematic; where the study is more broad or exploratory, notes may include sketches and notes of various aspects that relate to the research question. In some studies, other forms of data capture may supplement the researcher's notes, e.g., audio recording, still photos or video.

In summary, there is no single right way to conduct an observational study. The study design should be appropriate to the study aims, but it is also likely to be shaped by the expertise of the researcher (e.g., to what extent they can meaningfully participate in the situation), the structure and culture of the situation being observed, the resources available and even the personality of the researcher (e.g., what they feel comfortable observing). Furthermore, the way a study is conducted will often evolve over time as the researcher develops an understanding of the context and an ability to participate constructively in it.

Planning an observational study involves several steps. The first is to select the setting(s) for observation. Just as participants for an interview study are recruited based on selection criteria, so settings for observation are chosen based on their suitability for addressing the research questions, and this might involve elements of convenience as well as objective suitability. For example, for his MSc project (Rajkomar and Blandford, 2012), Rajkomar aimed to investigate the use of infusion pumps, which deliver intravenous medication, in intensive care. Negotiating access through our nearest hospital turned out not to be too difficult, so we did that; we are aware that the resulting analysis may only apply to the one hospital setup, but we did our best to present our method and findings in sufficient detail that they could be replicated in other healthcare settings to assess their generalisability. We return to the topic of generalisability in Chapter 8.

Another step is to determine what is to be documented in each observation. It is not possible to observe everything so some focus is needed. This focus may be shaped by extant theory and by the research question. For example, we have tested and extended DCog in several studies (Rajkomar and Blandford, 2012; Furniss et al., 2015; Rajkomar et al., 2015). Given a focus on the design or use of a particular technology, it is likely that an HCI study will focus on user interactions with that technology, or on the broader system of work that they are situated in.

It is also necessary, as discussed above, to agree on the role of the observer within the study setting. Most perspectives on research study the situation as an outsider looking in. Participant observation and action research involve the researcher playing a more active role in the context while also studying it. These research approaches are discussed in Chapter 6.

In any observational study, data needs to be gathered, through note taking, perhaps audio, image and video recording, and maybe from existing documentation. It may also be necessary to refine the focus of the study. For example, when studying the work of ambulance control and the role of technology within this, we came to recognise that situation awareness, and the ways in which the work system and technology supported it, was an important theme. As well as continuing to pay attention to their interactions with their information systems, we developed a more detailed focus on how the ambulance dispatchers maintained situation awareness and how the systems they were working with supported this (Blandford and Wong, 2004).

Whatever is observed, it is important that detailed notes are taken and that correspondingly detailed digital data is recorded so that analysis results in a rich and insightful description of the situation.

## 4.3    THINK-ALOUD

In some forms of observation, the researcher is clearly present, shaping the data gathering through the questions they ask; in contrast, in a traditional think-aloud study the researcher retreats into the background. Think-aloud involves the users of an interactive system articulating their thoughts as they work with that system. Think-aloud studies typically focus on the interaction with a particular interface, and so are well suited to identifying strengths and limitations of that interface as well as the ways that people undertake their tasks using the interface. Think-aloud is most commonly used in laboratory-based usability studies, but also has a valuable role in situated studies; for example, our observations of how lawyers interact with information on the Web (Makri et al., 2008a) involved the lawyers thinking aloud so that we could better understand their interactive behaviour and their rationale for that behaviour.

There are two important aspects of preparing participants to think aloud. One is instructing them in how to think aloud: participants might tell the researcher what they are doing while interacting with a system; it is more important that they should provide a "stream of consciousness" on what they are *thinking*. Depending on the focus and scope of the study, participants might be encouraged to focus their think-aloud verbalisations primarily on the interface and their interactions with it, or primarily on the broad work they are undertaking. It is often helpful for people to practice thinking aloud using another system before starting data gathering, particularly if the focus of interest is on their reactions to a new interface, so that by the time they start using it they are comfortable with thinking aloud.

The second aspect of preparation is what tasks people are instructed to complete. When gathering data for a qualitative study, it is most common to ask people to simply do their work while thinking aloud (this is obviously not a suitable approach to take if that work involves talking or interacting with other people!). For example, in several of our studies of how people interact with information (e.g., Makri et al., 2007; Makri et al., 2008a; Makri and Warwick, 2010), we have asked participants to choose their own tasks. These think-aloud studies were naturalistic in the sense that the tasks were intended to be as realistic as possible in an observational setting. As most of our participants were students, they would typically choose to find information for their dissertations. Practicing lawyers typically chose tasks that involved finding information related to a case they were working on. In other studies of information interaction, we have given specific tasks to users; for example, when we compared the support for exploratory search provided by three different search interfaces (Diriye et al., 2010), one of the specific tasks we set was for users to find a web page on human trafficking. Specific tasks are also often given to users when think-aloud is used for usability or user testing, or for studies of cognition. However, this is outside the scope of this book.

Thinking aloud does not come naturally to everyone, so participants may sometimes fall silent. When this happens, asking "what are you thinking?" or similar can be useful for prompting them to resume thinking aloud (without being too abrupt a reminder). Sometimes participants may be unusually chatty, which may distract them from the task(s). When this happens, politely steer the participant back to the task.

In traditional think-aloud approaches (e.g., Boren and Ramey, 2000; Ericsson and Simon, 1984), it is recommended that researcher interventions are kept to a minimum in an attempt to avoid the interventions changing what users subsequently say or do as they continue to interact with the system. However, Nørgaard and Hornbæk (2006) found that, when conducted in practice, think-aloud studies did not do this. While this can be viewed negatively, this need not necessarily be the case; in think-aloud studies aimed at understanding users' interaction behaviour and their rationale behind this behaviour, asking questions can be more useful than staying silent. McDonald et al. (2015) found that the most useful types of intervention a researcher can make during a think-aloud observation are those that sought participant explanations and opinions. Interventions aimed at seeking clarification about participants' actions were found to be less useful. The decision on whether, how and how often to intervene in a think-aloud study should be made by referring back to the purpose of the study and, ultimately, by asking oneself, "are the benefits of intervening in this way likely to outweigh the drawbacks?" Piloting the study allows the researcher to find out, and to amend their approach if necessary. As with most other data gathering techniques, there are many different ways to go about gathering data, and these are shaped by the interests of the researcher, the purpose of the study and the practicalities of the situation. Olmsted-Hawala et al. (2010) outline and compare several different think-aloud protocols that you may want to consider.

## 4.4    SEMI-STRUCTURED INTERVIEWS

While think-alouds are often effective ways to gather verbal data from participants about perceptions and use of technology, they are only possible when people do "work" in a fixed place and already have access to the technology of interest. When "work" is mobile, or when the focus is on people's perceptions rather than their actions, or infrequent events that are hard to observe, interviews (discussed in depth by Portigal, 2013) are often a more appropriate way of gathering data.

Interviews may be more or less structured; a completely structured interview is like a questionnaire in that all questions are pre-determined, although a variety of answers may be expected; a completely unstructured interview is more like a conversation, albeit one with a particular focus and purpose. Semi-structured interviews fall between these poles, in that many questions (or at least themes) will be planned ahead of time, but lines of enquiry will be pursued within the interview to follow up on interesting and unexpected avenues that emerge.

Interviews are best suited for understanding people's perceptions of and experiences with technology. People's ability to self-report facts accurately is limited; for example, in one study (Blandford and Rugg, 2002), we asked participants to tell us how they completed a routine task, and then to show us how they completed it. The practical demonstration revealed many steps and nuances that were absent from the verbal account: these details were taken for granted, so obvious that participants did not even think to mention them.

It is important to prepare carefully for interviews. One key step is recruiting suitable participants (discussed in the previous chapter). Another is planning the interview carefully (Arthur and Nazroo, 2003). Even though semi-structured interviews are less formal than structured ones, they are more than coffee shop chats: they have a purpose, and you will typically plan to cover several topics that address that purpose. This plan is called a topic guide, semi-structured interview script or interview guide. It should list topics to cover, and may include examples of possible questions that might be asked, or adapted. It can be useful to have prepared important questions verbatim—not because the question should be asked rigidly as prepared, but that it gives one way of asking it. This is particularly valuable if the researcher's mind goes blank during the interview. The topic guide should also serve as a plan for the interview, providing a logical order for covering topics. In practice, participants may introduce topics earlier than you plan, so the plan may change substantially. The overall plan for an interview would typically have the following structure:

1. **Opening the conversation:** It is important to put participants at their ease early on, and to assure them that they have expertise and experiences that you wish to understand.

2. **Introducing the research:** This involves ensuring that the participant is aware of the purpose of the research, and has given informed consent and understands their right to withdraw. It is also important to check whether they are happy to have the interview recorded.

3. **Beginning the interview:** The early stages usually focus on gathering background facts. This might include details about the participant's job or technology use. This can help with putting participants at their ease as well as contextualising the rest of the interview.

4. **During the interview:** The body of the interview will be shaped by the themes of interest for the research. HCI interviews are likely to involve participants focusing on issues surrounding the usability, usefulness and use of technology. These are likely to be topics they do not consider in such depth in their everyday lives; for many people, technology design and use are not the focus of their attention, except when it goes wrong. It can be helpful to have access to the technology during the interview, if this is possible.

5. **Closing the interview:** Participants should be given the chance to add anything else they want to say—e.g., on closely related topics, or things they forgot to say earlier. Many participants think of additional things to say once the recorder is off, and these may be noted. At the end, participants should be thanked and told what will happen next with

the data they provided. For example, the interview data may be used to inform future technology design. Participants are often glad to contribute to studies that aim to improve the technology they work with.

When interviewing, it is important to avoid leading questions and to make sure all questions are clear and succinct. It is often effective to employ a variety of strategies for questioning, including the use of broad and narrow questions. Try to use open rather than closed questions to invite detail. A useful technique for probing more detail is to echo the participant's words. For example, if the participant says, "I wish the information on this screen was clearer" and then goes silent, the researcher might say, "you wish the information was clearer?" This can invite the participant to provide more detail while demonstrating that the researcher is listening.

Within the core phase of interviewing, one technique to help with recall is the use of examples, asking people to focus on the details of specific incidents rather than generalisations. For example, the critical incident technique (Flanagan, 1954) can be used to elicit details of unusual and memorable past events. In the context of HCI, this might include times when a technology failed or when particular demands were placed on a system. A variant of this approach is the Critical Decision Method (Klein at al., 1989). In brief, this approach involves working with participants to reconstruct their thought processes while dealing with a problematic situation that involved working with partial knowledge and making difficult decisions. The Critical Decision Method helps to elicit aspects of expertise that are particularly well suited to studying technology use in high-pressure environments where the situation is changing rapidly and decisions need to be made, such as control rooms, operating theatres and flight decks.

When exploring future design possibilities, it is often useful to be very "grounded" to get at critical details that need to be understood for interaction design. Figure 4.1 shows some example questions that we devised for understanding women's needs for a decision support tool for making choices about contraception.

- Think back to the most recent (or the first) time you had to make a choice about contraception.

- What was it that caused you to review your choice of contraception?

- Talk me through how you made the decision: who did you talk with about it? What sources of information did you consult? Did you look online for information? Did you use any online tools to help you make a decision? Do you remember which ones?

- [If they used online resources]: What features of the resources did you find particularly helpful [ideally focusing on named resources if they can remember them]? Were there things they could have done better, or features that you'd have liked that weren't available?

- If you look ahead to the future, what do you think might prompt you to review your choice of contraception?

- Can you imagine any new kinds of online resources or apps that you'd like to see to help you make an informed choice? What might they be like?

Figure 4.1: Example questions to probe past experiences for the design of a future contraception decision support tool.

When planning for the design of future tools, it is important to understand the contexts in which people might choose to use them. To make the situation "real" for people, it is often effective to present detailed scenarios of use and invite people to critique them. An example from the same study is shown in Figure 4.2.

*Imagine the following situation:*

At your local chemist, they've installed a small, discreet booth (it looks a bit like a photo booth, except that it has neither photos nor signage on the outside) near the pharmacy counter. When you visit the chemist (for whatever reason), the shop assistant tells you that the booth is available for you if ever you wish to review your method of contraception, and hands you a short leaflet describing the decision support tools that you can access in the booth and inviting you to try it out. You step inside and draw the curtain. There, you find an interactive display that allows you to explore the benefits and limitations of a wide range of contraceptive methods, to express your values, to explore myths and truths about different methods, and to print out information about the methods you find most interesting, together with details of how to get access to each of those methods or where to go if you wish to discuss the options further. You spend about 10 minutes in the booth. When you step outside, you notice a couple of other women hovering around, apparently waiting to try out the booth for themselves.

*Could you imagine yourself doing this? What would prompt you to make use of such a resource? Would you feel comfortable about it? Would it be something you'd find a positive experience? Would it give you more confidence in your decision? How could it be improved?*

Figure 4.2: Example scenario from a study that focused on the design of a future contraception decision support tool.

Not all HCI studies are heavily directed towards informing design: some focus more on understanding people's experiences with technology, or on constructing models of technology use in practice. Charmaz (2014) describes an intensive interview as a "directed conversation." Her focus is on interviewing within GT, and on eliciting participants' experiences. She emphasises the importance of listening, of being sensitive, and of encouraging participants to talk, of asking open-ended questions and not being judgmental. Although the participant should do most of the talking, the interviewer will shape the dialogue, steering the discussion towards areas of research interest while attending less to areas that are out of scope. She emphasises the "contextual and negotiated" (p. 71) qualities of an interview: that the interviewer is a participant in shaping the conversation. Therefore, it is often important to reflect on the interviewer's role when analysing the data and reporting the outcomes of a study.

Legard et al. (2003) present two views of in-depth interviewing. One starts from the premise that knowledge is "given" and that the researcher's task is to dig it out. Although they do not use the term, this is in a positivist tradition. The other view is an interpretivist one, i.e., that knowledge is negotiated through the conversation between interviewer and interviewee. We describe these contrasting traditions in Chapter 6. Legard et al. emphasise the importance of building a relationship, noting that the interviewer is a "research instrument," but also that researchers need "a degree of humility, the ability to be recipients of the participant's wisdom without needing to compete by demonstrating their own" (p. 143). Some have introduced other instruments to complement how the interview and conversation is handled. For example, Blythe and colleagues used sketches and artwork as "tickets to talk" and "tickets to be silent" for people in a residential care home (Blythe et al., 2010). These acted as excuses to talk and afforded more comfortable silences within a shared space respectively. These metaphorical tickets could suit engagement with groups that are vulnerable, different from ourselves, and when discussing potentially sensitive non-work-related issues.

## 4.5    FOCUS GROUPS

Focus groups (e.g., Krueger and Casey, 2014) may be an alternative to interviews. However, they also have important differences. The researcher typically takes a role as facilitator but the main interactions are between participants, whose responses build on and react to each others'. The composition of a focus group can have a great effect on the dynamic and outcome in terms of data gathered. Sometimes a decision will be made to gather data through focus groups to exploit the positive aspects of group dynamics; at other times, the decision will be more pragmatic. For example, Adams et al. (2005) gathered data from individual practicing doctors through interviews, because these people typically had their own offices (a location for an interview), but also had very busy diaries, so that each interview had to be scheduled for a time when the participant was available (and many had to be delayed or rescheduled due to the demands of work). However, they gathered data from trainee nurses through focus groups because these people formed a cohort who knew each other reasonably well, and who often had breaks at the same time, so it was both easier and more productive to conduct focus groups than interviews.

Planning for a focus group has many similarities with planning for interviews, except that all people in the group need to be introduced, that questions cannot reasonably be so detailed or personal and that topics should be presented in a way that encourages open discussion between participants. It is usually a good idea to establish and agree to some rules at the beginning of the focus group to ensure that people are willing and able to express their views. For example, participants might be encouraged to take turns in speaking and to encourage others to speak so that everyone has a say. It is also useful to reassure participants that their views will remain confidential. Towards the end of the focus group, it is useful for the researcher to sum up key themes that arose to check that participants agree with the summary.

An important purpose of HCI focus groups is often to understand people's experiences with an existing technology and to elicit requirements for new or improved technology. Traditional HCI approaches such as personas and scenarios can be useful in supporting these types of focus groups. For example, when we were at the early stages of designing a "semantic sketchbook" mobile app that aimed to support users in making connections between people, places and information on the

Web, we ran a focus group with potential users of the app to elicit their requirements. In the focus group, we presented several personas and scenarios to illustrate potential uses of the app and then asked questions based on them. For example, one of the personas, Richard, was invited to provide the app with access to his calendar (in order for the app to suggest places he might want to visit when he was already in a particular area). We asked the focus group participants what would encourage and discourage them to provide the app with access to their calendars. While we received a variety of responses, we were able to converge on a consensus that nothing would completely reassure participants. We therefore decided against supporting this functionality in our subsequent designs. The personas and scenarios helped participants to better understand the implications of proposed design features.

## 4.6    DIARY STUDIES AND AUTOETHNOGRAPHY

Diary studies enable participants to record data in their own time, at particular times of day or when a particular trigger occurs. Diary entries may be more or less structured; for example, the Experience Sampling Method (Csikszentmihalyi and Larson, 2014; Consolvo and Walker, 2003) requires participants to report their current status in a short, structured form, often on their smartphones, whereas video diaries may allow participants to audio-record their thoughts, with accompanying video, with minimal structure. Kamsin et al. (2012) investigated people's time management strategies and tools using both interviews and video diaries. While interviews gave good insights into people's overall strategies and priorities, the immediacy of video diaries delivered a greater sense of the challenges that people faced in juggling the demands on their time and of the central role that email plays in many academics' time management. As an alternative to a video diary, it is possible to ask participants to capture their own images related to the focus of the research study, e.g., on their smartphones. These images can act as prompts for later interviews (e.g., Kindberg et al., 2005), where the researcher can ask participants for details about the images and why they were taken.

When planning a diary study, it is important to prepare clear instructions for participants, and to pilot test them with a few volunteers to make sure that they are not open to misinterpretation. When recruiting people to a diary study, it is common to plan an initial interview to introduce participants to the study and allow them to answer any questions they may have, and a debriefing interview to enable participants to reflect on their experiences and discuss the data in more detail. It is also often useful to recruit more diary study participants than you think you will need, as some will inevitably drop out or not record data as regularly as required.

Another approach that has been used occasionally to better understand user experience, particularly with mobile and personal devices, is autoethnography (Ellis et al., 2011; O'Kane et al., 2014). This is a form of diary study where the diary is kept by the researcher to record their experiences of living with a particular technology. For example, O'Kane "lived with" a wrist blood pressure monitor used by people with conditions such as hypertension. While a single person's experience cannot be considered representative of a broader population, it can be an excellent starting point. O'Kane et al. (2014) note that autoethnography can be a useful first step in user research as it can provide in-depth data and fresh insights that might help in planning subsequent studies with other participants.

Figure 4.3: Exemplar photos from an autoethnography (O'Kane et al., 2014), illustrating different contexts in which the researcher found herself measuring her blood pressure (a dark place, a washroom, an airport lounge, a restaurant, a café). Images courtesy of Aisling Ann O'Kane. Far left image from O'Kane et al. (2014). Used with permission.

## 4.7     WORKING WITH EXISTING SOURCES

There are some research questions that are best addressed by analysing existing sources. For example, reviews of mobile apps can provide an overview of what certain people think of the app, and published games reviews can provide insights into what features matter to games reviewers (Calvillo-Gamez et al., 2008). When working with existing textual sources, it is important to understand the limitations of those sources. Without knowledge of the authors or the ability to ask further questions, you are limited to the data as presented. It is also important to determine criteria for including and excluding particular text and to apply those criteria rigorously and transparently. For example, Rubin et al. (2010) analysed blog posts on Google Blog with a focus on finding potential examples of serendipity ("happy accidents"). They analysed only those blog posts that included one of several defined phrases in the blog text, e.g., "I had an aha moment" or "discovered…by accident."

Another useful source of data can be videos (e.g., from YouTube), particularly when there is existing data for contexts that may be hard to access, such as people's homes. For example, Paay et al. (2015) discuss the use of existing video material to study people's interactions while cooking. Similarly, Blythe and Cairns (2009) draw on user-generated content (particularly YouTube resources) to present an analysis of people's responses to a new smart phone, exploring the use of different analysis methods (the theme for the following chapter) to draw out insights from the data.

Figure 4.4: There are many different semi-structured qualitative methods and techniques that can be adopted and adapted to good effect. Different methods will be more or less suitable for different purposes.

## 4.8     SUMMARY AND CHECKLIST: DATA GATHERING

Researchers want to gather the most appropriate and best quality data that they can, so that the next stage (analysis) delivers valuable findings.

Checklist C summarises some of the issues that need to be considered when gathering data.

| Checklist C: Data gathering | |
|---|---|
| **Techniques for data gathering** | How will data be gathered (interviews, observation, etc.)? |
| | How will it be recorded? |
| | If multiple methods are to be used, how will they be sequenced and coordinated (see Chapter 6)? |
| | What role (if any) will theory play in data gathering? |
| | What protocol will be used for observations? What script will be used for semi-structured interviews? What participant instructions will be given for think-alouds? |
| | How will data gathering be timed, e.g., to sample particular kinds of activity? |
| | What is the likely relationship between interviewer and participant, and how is this likely to affect the data that is gathered? |
| | [Reflect:] Is the proposed data gathering method appropriate to the purpose of the study? |

# CHAPTER 5

# Analysing Data

## *THE EDITOR'S WORK*

Once the film footage has been gathered, then the editor's job is to organise and structure the footage to give a clear narrative and take-home message (journalists often call this the "angle" of a narrative). In ethnographic documentary making the specifics of the narrative are undecided until the footage has been reviewed, i.e., the themes emerge from the raw materials. The same is true of data analysis. This involves several iterations through the data to reorganise and structure it. In this chapter, for simplicity, we consider analysis independent of data gathering; in Chapter 6 we discuss interleaving of these activities.

## 5.1 FROM BUCKETS TO CAUSAL NARRATIVES: DIFFERENT APPROACHES TO CODING AND ANALYSING DATA

Most data for semi-structured qualitative studies (SSQSs) exist in the form of field notes, audio files, photographs and videos. The first step of analysis is generally to transform these into a form that is easier to work with, e.g., transcribing audio, annotating or coding video. This may be done at different levels of detail, e.g., selectively transcribing text that is directly relevant to the theme of the study through to a full transcription of all words, phatic utterances, pauses and intonations. Oliver et al. (2005) argue that the act of transcription has an important effect on the outcome of analysis; while this is undoubtedly true, the approach to transcription should be guided by the purpose of the study. For HCI studies, it is most common to transcribe all words, and often phatic utterances (ums, errs, etc.) but not pauses or intonations, as the focus of analysis is most commonly on articulated rather than more nuanced meaning. Some researchers choose to transcribe data themselves, as the very act of transcribing is a useful step in becoming familiar with the data and getting immersed in it. Making notes as you transcribe can enhance this. Others prefer to pay a good typist to transcribe data because this might get the transcription done more quickly and less painfully; it typically takes 4–6 hours to transcribe an hour of audio.

An identifying feature of SSQSs is that they involve some form of coding of the data. This involves identifying units of data (e.g., single words, phrases, extended utterances, objects featuring in photographs, actions noted in videos, etc.) and giving these useful descriptors or labels. Abstract codes help spot themes and patterns in the data. Coded units can be compared and contrasted to construct an analytical narrative based on the data. Grounded Theory and Thematic Analysis (as described below) exemplify structured ways of coding data for analysis. All approaches to coding aim to help researchers organise their data in order to make sense of it, just like reorganising Scrabble letters can help players see words they may not have noticed previously (Figure 5.1).

Figure 5.1: Organising data can help with identifying patterns in that data.

The coding process often results in us seeing our findings from a new and more abstract perspective. Common activities in the coding process include:

- **creating** new codes;

- **renaming** existing codes, e.g., when you find a more accurate, precise or elegant way of describing a code or when a new finding triggers you to re-think the scope of a code;

- **splitting** codes, when you decide that a theme in the data is more usefully described as two distinct themes;

- **merging** codes, when you decide that two themes in the data are not as distinct as you previously thought and therefore combine them;

- creating **hierarchies** of codes, to help understand how the codes relate to one another and aid writing up. These code hierarchies can subsequently be used as headings and sub-headings to structure and explain your findings; and

- creating **links** between codes that are related in ways other than hierarchical. This can be enlightening and lead to a richer picture of the phenomena and system being studied. For example, attending to process could describe stages of a design process, how someone develops expertise, a user's journey in discovering information, or coming to terms with a disease. This contrasts with a hierarchical description which is restricted to linking categories to sub-categories, e.g., linking "user-testing," "cognitive walkthrough," and "heuristic evaluation" to "usability evaluation methods," or linking "happy," "sad," and "frustrated" to "emotions."

This final step can make the difference between a staccato set of paragraphs and a compelling account that makes sense of the data in a rich and revealing way.

## 5.2    A PRAGMATIC APPROACH TO ANALYSIS

So, you have some data. It might just be a couple of interview transcripts, or it might represent many hours of observational data. Where do you start with analysis? The following is an intentionally informal and practical description of one approach; more formal and detailed approaches are discussed later.

For manageable quantities of data, a pragmatic approach for "bottom-up" or "grounded" qualitative data analysis is to start with improvised tools such as colored pens and lots of notebooks, or a simple word processor file, and to do a first pass of approximate coding (either using the annotation feature or in a multi-column table). At that stage, it is not necessary to worry about consistency of codes; the aim is just to see what is in the data, what seem to be the common patterns and themes, and what are the surprises that might be worth looking at in more detail. You will typically focus on the sentence level. On a second pass through all the data, you can start to look systematically for the themes that seem most interesting or promising for analysis. If you have a large quantity of data, you might choose to copy-and-paste relevant chunks of text into a separate document organised according to the themes, without worrying about connections between the themes. If this is done, it is important to annotate each chunk with which participant it came from so that it is easy to retrieve the context for each quotation. It is important to review the whole corpus of data, not just these edited highlights, in subsequent stages of analysis. It is also important to step back to review the big picture periodically: are there patterns (e.g., groupings) in the codes, and are the detailed themes consistent with the overall narrative of the data? You iterate between detail and big picture to make sure that you are getting the details right while also getting the big picture coherent. The next step is to build a narrative within each of the themes. At this point, you may realise that there are other data that also relate to a theme that you had not noticed on the previous passes, so you might revise the themes and the narrative. The next step is to develop a meta-narrative that links the themes together into an overall story. At this point, some themes will be removed and others become the focus of attention; maybe you will realise that there is another theme in the data that should be part of this bigger narrative, so you may need to revise the narrative again, or even return to re-code some of the data. Repeat until done! Although this sounds chaotic, it should become highly systematic and rigorous in later stages. In the later stages you should be intimately familiar with the data, and with tiny nuances within it. For your chosen themes, you should be confident that all the data that relates to those themes have been taken into account, whether it clearly supports the argument or raises interesting contradictions. Where data seem to contradict emerging themes, it is important to understand why. It is likely that you have over-simplified your account, and that it needs refining. It is also important to be aware of the absence of data that you might expect. If a particular interview participant has not mentioned a theme that is clearly important to others, is that because the interview went off in a different direction or because that theme is really not important to that participant? If the latter, then you clearly cannot claim that all participants agreed that the theme was important.

It can be easy to overlook nuances in the data. For example, several years ago, when we were studying how people interacted with health information, we identified an "information journey" (Adams and Blandford, 2005), with three main stages: recognising an information need; gathering information and interpreting that information. The important point (to us) was highlighting the importance of interpretation. The dominant view of information seeking at that time was that if people could find information then that was the end of the story. However, we found that an important role for clinicians is in helping lay people to interpret clinical information in terms of what it means for that individual. In later studies of lawyers' information work (Makri et al., 2008a), we realised that there were two important elements missing from the information journey as we had formulated it. The first was information validation, and the second was information use. When we looked back at the health data, we did not see a lot of evidence of validation. It might have been there, but it was largely implicit, and rolled up with interpretation. However, now sensitised to it, we found a lot of evidence of information use. Of course people use the information they find, e.g., to manage their health conditions, but we simply had not noticed it because people did not talk explicitly about it as "using" the information. This is an example of conceptual refinement.

At some point, you relate the themes you have found to the existing literature. Where that point is will vary from study to study. In some cases, the literature review will have guided all the data gathering and analysis. In other cases, you think you have finished your analysis, realise that someone has already written a paper with similar findings to yours, utter a few expletives and review what alternative narratives there might be in your data that are equally well-founded but more novel. Usually, it is somewhere between these extremes. Sometimes your findings may be related to existing literature you were not previously aware of or did not think would have important implications for your findings. For example, in our study of how architects interact with information (Makri and Warwick, 2010), we found that they often *encountered* (stumbled upon) information they were not specifically looking for when searching Google Images. The information they stumbled upon often helped them to make creative design decisions, e.g., about how a particular building they were planning should look. This led us to examine and relate our findings to existing literature on "information encountering" (e.g., Erdelez, 2004) and on creativity and design (e.g., Shneiderman, 2001). Although we had the choice of introducing the existing work in our literature review, we decided instead to relate our findings to this literature in the "discussion" section of our paper as we felt we could not have anticipated the importance of information encountering or creativity in our study, which aimed to understand architects' broad information interaction behaviour rather than these particular aspects of it. The link to literature and theory is discussed in Chapter 6, and decisions about how to write up in Chapter 7. We discuss Thematic Analysis as an analysis method below, and Grounded Theory as a particular approach to qualitative research in Chapter 6.

Figure 5.2: One of the challenges of analysing qualitative data is to pay special attention to the nuances and details of the data, but not get too lost, and then represent this data as a more abstract pattern or show some more higher-level insight. This means frequent engagement with details and abstractions.

## 5.3    TOOLS FOR QUALITATIVE DATA ANALYSIS

If you only have a few hours of data to analyse, it is possible to keep track of it well with the informal tools discussed above. When the dataset gets larger, this becomes impossible, and analysis is best supported by the use of a Qualitative Data Analysis (QDA) tool such as ATLAS.ti, MaxQDA, NVivo or Dedoose. Any tool creates mediating representations between the analyst and the data, allowing the researcher to organise and make sense of the data. Decisions about whether to use a QDA tool and which one to use may be based on prior experience, on the size and manageability of the dataset, on the availability of a constant Internet connection and on personal preference. One researcher may choose to use a set of tables in a word processor or to print it out and annotate with colored pens. Another might use sticky notes to create an affinity diagram where concepts are written out on notes, maybe using color to signify different kinds of concepts, and the notes are organised and re-organised into themes (e.g., Harboe et al., 2012). Digital QDA tools are particularly useful for helping researchers manage large bodies of data, where it would be difficult or impossible to organise the data manually. They are also useful for helping to ensure coding consistency. All offer the ability to create and maintain a list of codes and to create new codes. This makes inconsistencies in code labelling easy to notice and correct, and makes inconsistencies difficult to create in the first place.

One of the most useful functionalities supported by most QDA tools is allowing researchers to read or export a group of quotations that they have assigned a particular code to. This can support both analysis and reporting. Looking over all instances of a code can provide new insights into the nature or boundaries of the subject matter covered by that code. It can also aid the researcher in asking questions of the data, such as "is this the most appropriate name for this code?", "does this code really fit this quotation?" and "are there any other quotations that should be included under this particular code?" Researchers should not try to discover and make use of every feature of a QDA tool. Instead they should use digital tools only as far as they support them in doing their analysis efficiently and effectively and in generating useful insights from the data.

Other analytic tools that can help the analysis process include diaries, memos and network diagrams. The process of being immersed in qualitative analysis can be absorbing, and it can be hard to remember the analytical moves you made, what you have learnt and where you have come from in terms of assumptions and learning. Keeping a diary of your progress and thoughts can help track this. Memos are a flexible form of note taking that can provide a useful supplement to the coding process. Do not get too absorbed in creating codes; after all, this is just a means to an end, which is making sense of the data and gaining insights. Memos can be a means to these ends too. Network diagrams are visual representations of how codes link together and relate to each other. This can help think about codes in an abstract way, in different groups, arrangements and processes. Again, network diagrams and other visual forms of representations may provide analytical tools to help you make sense of your data.

Whatever QDA tool you choose to use (or not), sensemaking is your responsibility, so there is no substitute for the power of your own mind. You collected and perhaps transcribed the data and therefore have good familiarity with it. An old adage goes: "a wise man can see more from the bottom of a well than a fool can from a mountain top." Just as sophisticated documentary editing tools do not guarantee the creation of an interesting documentary, QDA tools do not guarantee useful insights. They support you in creating your own insights.

## 5.4    THEMATIC ANALYSIS

Our description of analysis thus far has not named it as a specific method, but has presented it as a practical process, focusing on the tools and the moves that are made in analysis. There are various more formal descriptions of this process; as noted earlier, the term "Grounded Theory" is widely used to refer to a generic QDA approach, though it also has a more precise meaning as described in Chapter 6. Other terms and techniques include the Framework Method (Gale et al., 2013), Emergent Themes Analysis (Wong and Blandford, 2002) and Thematic Analysis (TA: Braun and Clarke, 2006). These different terms describe very similar approaches, and different detailed descriptions of the same named method are at least as different as descriptions of methods with different names. They all assume that data has already been collected, and focus on how that data is to be analysed. We focus in particular on TA as described by Braun and Clarke (2006). They argue that "thematising meanings" is a generic skill across qualitative methods and that TA builds directly on this skill. They contrast TA with qualitative techniques such as conversation analysis or interpretative phenomenological analysis (both rarely used in HCI), which are founded on a particular theoretical position and are typically applied in relatively tightly defined ways. Rather, they place TA in a camp of techniques that can be applied across a range of theoretical positions, and that tries to steer a path between "anything goes" unstructured analysis and an approach that is overly constrained. They make the obvious but key point that "What is important is that the theoretical framework and methods match what the researcher wants to know, and that they acknowledge these decisions, and recognise them as decisions" (p. 80). Other descriptions of TA emphasise different features of the approach; for example, Joffe (2012) focuses much more on agreeing a set of codes and having multiple independent coders. Joffe's approach is much more quantitative, and sits more comfortably in a positivist research tradition, although the basic approach is largely similar.

Braun and Clarke (2006, p. 87) identify six phases of TA.

1. **Familiarising yourself with the data:** simply reading and re-reading the data, making notes of ideas that spring to mind.

2. **Generating initial codes:** coding the entire dataset systematically and collating data that is relevant to each code. They define codes as labels that "identify a feature of the data (semantic content or latent) that appears interesting to the analyst" (p. 88).

3. **Searching for themes:** gathering codes (and related data) into candidate themes for further analysis.

4. **Reviewing themes:** checking whether the themes work with the data and creating a thematic map of the analysis.

5. **Defining and naming themes:** refining the themes and the overall narrative iteratively.

6. **Producing the report:** which will, in turn require a further level of reflection on the themes, the narrative and the examples used to illustrate themes.

These phases represent an approach to iteratively deepening engagement with the data through layers of analysis. This is essentially a formalised version of the pragmatic approach presented in the previous section.

Consistent with their overall flexible approach, Braun and Clarke (2006) are not prescriptive about whether an analysis should be informed or driven by a particular theory or primarily by the data: "Coding will, to some extent, depend on whether the themes are more 'data-driven' or 'theory-driven'—in the former, the themes will depend on the data, but in the latter, you might approach the data with specific questions in mind that you wish to code around" (p. 88–89). This is a theme to which we return in Chapter 6.

## 5.5 ILLUSTRATIVE EXAMPLE

To illustrate three steps in analysis, we take short excerpts from two transcripts of interviews gathered to understand people's experiences of working in physical libraries; these interviews were conducted to better understand requirements for the design of digital libraries. Our initial focus was on the practicalities: how people located and used resources in the library. However, it quickly became evident that people also had strong emotional responses to particular libraries, so this became a further focus for analysis.

Figure 5.3 illustrates initial coding of excerpts from two different transcripts. At this stage, we have simply highlighted appearance of the word "love" and underlined phrases that indicate an emotional response (positive or negative) to being in a particular space.

---

R1: "*When I was a graduate student I **loved** working in Library A because it is such a **lovely** place to work. The difficulty here is—I <u>hate</u> working in Library B, I think it's a slum; it's an airport lounge, erm, I <u>can't stand</u> Library C which is even more of a slum; I <u>don't care for</u> Library D very much, so I don't like working there. But when I go abroad—I've just been to Washington; working in Library E there is <u>very pleasant</u> and I <u>enjoy</u> that, although you don't get much done because people come and talk to you and show you things, there's chat and you can't do long stints, at Library E, at 3:45 they ring a bell and you have to go and have tea.*"

R2: "*I **love** Library B to work in, it's <u>a pain in the arse</u> to get things out, because you know, you, everything is, you know, you have to go and order it, but its thirty minutes minimum you know, but I **love** going in there, sitting in there and working in there. I think <u>it's just amazing</u> as a building and I never really thought about the extent to which <u>the environment affects me</u>.*"

---

Figure 5.3: Initial coding of data, highlighting positive and negative statements.

In the same transcripts, we realised that the feelings that were being expressed related, both positively and negatively, to the environment as perceived by participants, and to their sense of productivity in that space. The next layer of annotation is illustrated in Figure 5.4 (in practice, the initial annotation was done with colored pens rather than by using different fonts).

> R1: *When I was a graduate student I* `loved` `working` *in Library A because it is such a lovely place to work. The difficulty here is—I* `hate` *working in Library B, I think it's a* **`slum`**; *it's an* **`airport` `lounge`**, *erm, I* `can't` `stand` *Library C which is even more of a* **`slum`**; *I* `don't` `care` *for Library D very much, so I* `don't` `like` `working` *there. But when I go abroad—I've just been to Washington; working in Library E there is* `very` `pleasant` *and* **`I` `enjoy` `that`**, *although you don't get much done because people come and talk to you and show you things,* **`there's` `chat`** *and you can't do long stints, at Library E, at 3:45 they ring a bell and you have to go and have tea."*
>
> R2: "*I love Library B to work in, it's* `a` `pain` `in` `the` `arse` *to get things out, because you know, you, everything is, you know, you have to go and order it, but its thirty minutes minimum you know, but I* `love` *going in there, sitting in there and working in there. I think* `it's` `just` `amazing` *as a building and I never really thought about* **`the` `extent` `to` `which` `the` `environment` `affects` `me`**."

Figure 5.4: The same transcripts, analysed in more depth. Here, we us different fonts to highlight phrases referring to `feelings`, the **`environment`** and *productivity*.

This coding led us to ask further questions of the data, which could have been followed up in further interviews had we taken this study further. Questions included:

- What is this work?

- What are the requirements of the work?

- What does respondent R1 mean by slum and airport lounge?

- Who comes to talk to R1?

- What is special about 3:45? What is R1's normal working schedule?

- In what way does the environment influence them? Being productive or enjoyment?

This short example gives a flavour of how you might approach data analysis. For any given dataset, a full analysis involves getting immersed in that data to perceive nuances that might not have been immediately apparent. Texts such as Charmaz (2014) include more extended examples.

## 5.6 TOP-DOWN APPROACHES TO ANALYSIS

In this book, we are focusing on semi-structured interpretive approaches to qualitative research—i.e., where codes are identified from the data rather than being pre-defined. It is rare for HCI studies to start with pre-determined codes unless they are strongly shaped by a particular theoretical perspective from the outset. Miles and Huberman (1994) present an extensive discussion of top-down approaches to qualitative data analysis.

## 5.7   SUMMARY AND CHECKLIST: ANALYSING DATA

Like the editor of a documentary film, your aim should be to construct as accurate and compelling an account of what you have found from your data as possible. This might be as simple as a set of requirements or scenarios for a future system design, or it might be a rich causal narrative to account for people's interactions with and around technology. Although qualitative data analysis is time-consuming, more often than not the time you invest in really getting to know the data will pay off in the form of interesting new insights. These insights will allow you to construct a convincing, coherent narrative, strongly supported by evidence from the data.

Checklist D summarises some of the issues that need to be considered in analysis.

| Checklist D: Analysing data | |
|---|---|
| **Data analysis** | How will data be analysed? |
| | At what level of detail will transcription take place? |
| | What tools will be used to support analysis? |
| | Will codes be pre-determined or will they be determined during analysis? |
| | Will coding be done individually or by multiple people? If there are multiple coders, is their coding independent or negotiated? |
| | If the analysis is individual and reflexive, what steps will the researcher take to ensure the validity of findings? |
| | Will participants be involved in analysis and/or validation? If so, how? See Chapter 8 for more details. |

# CHAPTER 6

# Paradigms and Strategies

## *USING APPROPRIATE FILMIC CONVENTIONS*

Documentaries on different topics generally exploit different filmic devices such as talking heads, voice-overs, cameras shadowing people, aerial shots, etc. Particular techniques suit certain approaches and endeavours. For example, voice-overs go well with wildlife documentaries whereas interviewing wild animals makes little sense. Conversely, aerial shots can be very effective if discussing migrations of herds, but are less likely to be useful for illustrating the latest science in genomics. Similarly, in HCI studies, it is important to select an approach that is appropriate to the aims of the study. There should be coherence between the purpose, paradigm, strategy, approach, technique, etc.

Understanding factors that can shape qualitative studies allows HCI researchers to find ways of conducting research for each project, with its own unique aims, objectives, resources and constraints. Some studies will be shaped as they progress, and as understanding of the situation evolves. Others will be designed from the outset as multi-phase studies. In this section, we review different dimensions and factors that influence the shape and style of studies:

- **research paradigms:** this is background material for the interested reader (particularly the quantitative researcher) to locate semi-structured qualitative studies (SSQSs) within the space of empirical research paradigms that are common in HCI;

- **research strategies:** in Chapters 4 and 5 we presented particular techniques for gathering and analysing data; these are generally selected through a research strategy that shapes what is done to achieve the research objectives;

- the use of **mixed methods**; and

- **responding** to the situation.

## 6.1 RESEARCH PARADIGMS

To understand how various factors can shape semi-structured qualitative studies in HCI, we situate SSQSs among different styles of empirical research. There is a continuum of approaches to empirical research, from quantitative hypothesis-testing, through structured qualitative techniques such as content analysis (Kippendorff, 1980), to the semi-structured qualitative methods that have been the focus of this book, and the kinds of ethnography where insights are derived from the expertise of the researcher with little inspectable analysis (Figure 6.1). This section does not help you decide what to do in your particular study, but might help you determine whether doing a SSQS is appropriate in the first place.

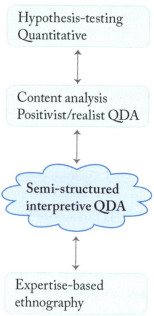

Figure 6.1: A continuum of styles of qualitative analysis, varying by their degree of structure. The focus of this book is the "cloud" area. Note that this is a continuum, not a hierarchy.

Quantitative research is most commonly applied to test pre-determined hypotheses. Quantitative studies based on statistical significance are widely regarded as the "gold standard" for hypothesis-driven research. In studies of people and interactions, they are invaluable for testing hypotheses regarding human cognition and its impact on people's interactions with technology. For example, we have conducted controlled experiments to better understand the cognitive factors and interface features that account for certain classes of human error (Li et al., 2008; Ament et al., 2013). They can also be useful for comparing measurements such as completion times, completion rates and errors between different interfaces and technologies.

Qualitative approaches typically address different types of questions to quantitative research. Rather than testing hypotheses, they are concerned with describing and explaining phenomena in a rich, often exploratory, way. While quantitative HCI studies address hypothesis-driven research questions such as "do users make fewer errors when interacting with one medical device than another?" or "does task complexity influence users' skim-reading behaviour when interacting with information?," qualitative HCI studies often address broader, exploratory questions such as "what different types of errors do users make when interacting with a novel medical device and why?" or "does task complexity influence users' information interaction behaviour and, if so, in what ways?" Qualitative HCI studies typically focus on the "whats" and "whys" of interaction. They address what users do when interacting with technology (their interactive behaviour) and why they do it (the rationale behind their behaviour), in order to inform design. While qualitative and quantitative approaches typically address different types of question, they often complement each other in "mixed methods" studies. For example, a qualitative exploration of a particular type of interaction behaviour such as types of errors made when interacting with a novel medical device might yield interesting insights, e.g., identifying a new kind of error not previously discussed in the literature. A quantitative study might then be conducted to examine the prevalence of this new type of error, thereby determining the generalisability of the qualitative findings. Conversely, a quantitative study might yield a surprising finding that could then be explored in depth in a follow-up qualitative study.

Structured approaches to qualitative data analysis include Content Analysis (Kippendorff, 1980) and positivist approaches to TA (e.g., Joffe, 2012). Positivist and realist approaches to data analysis assume that there is an objective reality "out there," and that the role of the analyst is to discover and present that reality in an unbiased way. Positivist approaches to data analysis assume, for example, that two independent analysts should be able to code the data in the same way and reach the same conclusions. If the data has been gathered from a suitably representative group of participants in a sufficiently standardised way then it becomes meaningful to count and report the number of instances of each code in the data. Typically, in this tradition, the codes to be applied to the data have to be pre-determined and precisely defined so that independent coders have a good shared understanding of their meanings prior to coding the data. Codes may have been pre-agreed even before the study commenced, or may have been derived from a preliminary analysis of the data. Inter-rater reliability techniques, to check the agreement between raters (Hallgren, 2012), are applicable here.

This book has focused on interpretivist semi-structured approaches. This is the most common type of qualitative approach applied in HCI research. Interpretivist approaches assume a subjective (rather than objective) reality that is constructed through the interpretations of researchers, study participants, and even readers of the research when written up. Interpretivist approaches emphasise the interpretation process in how we make sense of reality; these are closely related to constructivist approaches, which emphasise how we construct and create versions of reality. Many people use these terms interchangeably and avoid the deeper philosophical discourses around the distinction. Importantly, they both contrast with positivist approaches that assume it is possible to discover an external reality. Interpretivist approaches start at the very beginning of the study because we are already making decisions that influence our interpretation of the question, our approach, who to recruit, what data to gather, etc. Although common themes will be addressed across data-gathering sessions (whether those are interviews, observations or a combination of both), the semi-structured nature means that themes will be covered to different degrees depending on what the most fruitful lines of enquiry are. Whereas for positivist approaches it is important that agreement between researchers can be achieved, and it can be meaningful to report the number of instances of particular codes in the data, in interpretivist approaches it is recognised that researchers will have different backgrounds and biases and will therefore interpret qualitative data differently. While issues of researcher agreement are not so important in interpretivist approaches, this does not mean there should be researcher *disagreement* if multiple researchers were to analyse the same data. They should arrive at complementary, non-contradictory interpretations of that data even though they may be different in detail. In interpretivist approaches, it is particularly important that the data collection and analysis methods, as well as researcher interpretations of the data, are inspectable by others. This is to allow others to comprehend the journey from an initial question to a conclusion, so that they can assess its validity and generalisability and build on the research in an informed way. In this case, counting instances is rarely meaningful, and might be misleading, e.g., the first interviewees might have had different questions to interviewees later in the study. Instead, vaguer statements such as "one participant," "several participants" or "most participants commented" are common.

At the other end of the continuum, in terms of inspectability and structure, lie approaches to ethnography such as those described by Randall and Rouncefield (2013). Ethnography (like GT) is a term that has lost its meaning through over-use. The term "ethnography" has been widely adopted to refer to any kind of field method based on observation, but is also still used by some in a more powerful way to refer to the researcher "participating, overtly or covertly, in people's lives for an extended period of time" (Hammersley and Atkinson, 2007, p. 3). According to Randall and Rouncefield (2013), ethnography is not a stepwise method at all but "a qualitative orientation to research that emphasises the detailed observation of people in naturally occurring settings." They say, "we aim to collect data in as reasonable a fashion as we can, using whatever material is to be found and—because we have no claims to methodological purity—are careful to limit our analytic claims about the world to what we have seen and can reasonably infer." Also, that data gathering "will be dictated not by strategic methodological considerations, but by the flow of activity within the social setting." Blomberg and Burrell (2009) highlight that ethnography is based on an underlying assumption that in order to gain an understanding of a world they have little previous knowledge of, researchers must gain this understanding first-hand, e.g., through in-depth observation. According to Blomberg and Burrell, ethnographers are "interested in gaining an insider's view of a situation," attempting to view the world "from the perspective of the people studied." Anderson (1994) emphasises the role of the ethnographer as someone with an interpretive eye, delivering an account of patterns observed. He argues that while ethnography often involves fieldwork, not all fieldwork is ethnography and not everyone can be an ethnographer, as fieldwork requires a complex set of social, practical and interpersonal skills. In the ethnographic tradition (e.g., Heath and Luff, 1991; Vom Lehn and Heath, 2005), the moves that the researcher makes between observing the situation of interest and reporting findings often remain undocumented as these moves are difficult to ascertain or articulate when the researcher is so embedded in the situation and engaging with it in an unstructured, non-predetermined manner. This, however, means that precise details of data analysis are often unavailable to the interested or critical reader.

## 6.2    RESEARCH STRATEGIES

In all studies, data gathering and analysis are shaped by research aims. For example, there is little value in observing the colors of people's socks or what they eat for lunch if your focus is on how they enter data from a paper record into an online system unless there is some reason to believe that these are linked—in which case, the research would probably focus on that link.

### 6.2.1    BASING A STUDY ON A PARTICULAR THEORETICAL PERSPECTIVE

As discussed in Chapter 3, some studies adopt a particular theoretical perspective from the outset. The theory then shapes both the data gathering and the analysis. For example, one of our aims in a study of serendipity and creativity (Makri et al., 2014) was to validate an empirical model of serendipity with creative practitioners. Our interviews with creatives were shaped by the existing model; we asked questions to probe each aspect of it. But we also actively tried to minimise confirmation bias in the data gathered; we asked for more detail when the creatives mentioned something outside the scope of the model (to potentially extend or refine the model). We also asked them for counter-examples to test the validity of the model. We knew that interesting findings might arise where the model did *not* fit well with or did not fully explain their experiences. This led to the expansion of part of the model to incorporate actions the creatives took to "make their own luck" (strategies they thought made serendipity more likely to happen to them).

Similarly, Rajkomar et al. (2015) set out with two main intentions. The first was to understand how people stay safe on home haemodialysis; this is a complex and risky procedure for managing chronic kidney disease. The second was to test whether DiCoT could usefully be applied to better understand people's practices in the home environment, and particularly their safety practices. As noted earlier, DiCoT is an approach to analysing a system in terms of DCog (Hollan et al., 2000). Some of Rajkomar's planned interview questions explicitly covered what strategies people had developed for staying safe, what difficulties they had experienced, and their broader experiences of being on home haemodialysis. Given the focus on DCog, his observation notes and photographs focused largely on physical structures and how information was recorded and kept. This included both their explicit information records, such as phone numbers listed on a pin-board within easy view, and their implicit creation of information resources, such as a house key being kept in sight on a windowsill, ready to be thrown out to a neighbour in case of emergency (Figure 6.2).

Figure 6.2: A strategy for staying safe on home haemodialysis - leaving a key on a windowsill, ready to throw down to a neighbour in an emergency,

## 6.2.2    THEORY SHAPING ANALYSIS

Theory shaped the data gathering in the example above. In other cases it may not be explicitly used to shape data gathering, but might inform subsequent analysis. For example, Furniss et al. (2011a) were already familiar with the theory of DCog (Hollan et al., 2000; Furniss and Blandford, 2006), and although DCog was not used for structuring data gathering, we thought it would be a useful framework for exploring our data further, providing a "theoretical lens" on the analysis. In our case we found that it provided leverage to explore the data in a new way, beyond our initial GT analysis of the data. Theory can be used for secondary analyses of collected data.

Driven more by a need to make sense of data that was difficult to account for, Adams et al. (2005) explicitly searched for a theory that helped to account for their findings: we had studied several different digital library (DL) deployment projects and found that making DLs more accessible to healthcare practitioners (by making them available through shared computers in the workplace) reduced their use when it was expected to increase it. Conversely, a project which had placed clinical librarians as members of multi-disciplinary care teams had increased use of DLs. Theories such as DCog and Activity Theory (Kaptelinin, 2013) were explored, but did not help in accounting for our data. After some searching, we came across the theory of Communities of Practice (Wenger, 1998), which resonated with our data and felt like a delightful "lightbulb" moment. The theory helped us

to make sense of our data in a way that moved us from some interesting but idiosyncratic findings that were only relevant to our particular study contexts to findings that had some generalisability, and hence could be applied in other settings where new technology is being deployed.

Sometimes, the research aim changes, as you discover that your initial aim or assumptions about what you might find are wrong. This has happened to us more than once. For example, we conducted a study of London Underground control rooms (Smith et al., 2009). The initial aim was to understand the contrasts across different control rooms, what effects these differences had on the work of controllers, and the ways they used the various artefacts in the environment. In practice, we found that the commonalities were much more interesting than the contrasts and several themes emerged across contexts. The most intriguing was discovering that some controllers described themselves as playing with a train set. We discovered that although controllers take their job seriously there were aspects that linked to playing games, like solving puzzles and using exploratory learning. This links in to the literature on serious games, a literature that we had not even considered when we started the study (so we had to learn about it fast).

### 6.2.3    ETHNOMETHODOLOGY

One approach to weaving a particular perspective throughout a study that has been applied to the study of technology use in practice is "ethnomethodologically informed ethnography" (Button and Sharrock, 2009). Ethnomethodology studies the methods people use to make sense of the world and accomplish tasks, i.e., it is an approach to study in which "members' reasoning and methods for accomplishing situations becomes the topic of enquiry" (Crabtree et al., 2000, p. 666). This provides a particular focus on the people (the workers) within the study setting, how they make sense of their work, and the ways they use technology to support their work. The focus is on describing the work in all its mundane details, representing the perspective of the workers, without theorising but telling it as it is. Button and Sharrock (2009) take these ideas to present five maxims for conducting ethnomethodological studies of work: keep close to the work; examine the correspondence between work and the scheme of work; look for troubles great and small; take the lead from those who know the work; and identify where the work is done. They emphasise the importance of paying attention, not jumping to conclusions, valuing observation over verbal report and keeping comprehensive notes. The aim is to develop rich description to guide the design of future systems for those workers. Many of these principles apply to observational studies more generally; the ethnomethodological focus determines what the observer is attending to, namely the workers and how they use technology to make sense of their work.

### 6.2.4    CONTEXTUAL INQUIRY

As noted above, observations are usefully complemented by interviews. In HCI, the most widely reported approach to integrating observations and interviews is Contextual Inquiry (Beyer and Holtzblatt, 1998). As with several other terms, some people use "Contextual Inquiry" to refer to any approach that involves interleaving observations and interviews within the work setting; here we focus on the more specific description provided by Beyer and Holtzblatt (1998).

Contextual Inquiry is a method for conducting and recording observational studies in HCI as a stage in a broader process of Contextual Design. According to Holtzblatt and Beyer (2013), "Contextual Design prescribes interviews that are not pure ethnographic observations, but involve the user in discussion and reflection on their own actions, intents, and values." In other words, Contextual Inquiry involves interleaving observation with focused, situated interview questions concerning the work at hand and the roles of technology in that work. Questions will generally focus on how the technology does, or could, support the ongoing work. Questions might include "Who do you have to liaise with to get that sorted out?", "What tool do you use to achieve that?", "When does your colleague send you that information?", "Where do you store that information?" "Why does that form field flash red?", "How often do have to sort out problems like that one?", etc. The interleaving of observation and conversation helps to build a richer understanding of the work and how technology might be designed to support it better.

Holtzblatt and Beyer (2013) present five models (flow, cultural, sequence, physical and artefact) that are intermediate representations to describe work and the work context, and for which Contextual Inquiry is intended to provide data. Although Contextual Inquiry is often regarded as a component of Contextual Design, it has been applied independently as an approach to data gathering in research. For example, Blandford and Wong (2004) conducted Contextual Inquiry interviews in ambulance control, interleaving interviews and observations to understand the work of ambulance controllers and the way their computer systems supported their work.

### 6.2.5    PARTICIPANT OBSERVATION AND ACTION RESEARCH

Participant observation and action research both involve the researcher getting involved in the study setting while also gathering data about that setting.

In participant observation (Atkinson and Hammersley, 1994), the researcher might have particular skills and knowledge that they bring to a group, which legitimises their active role in the group, and they can study it at the same time. Part-time MSc students have used this approach when they have particular roles through their employment, which gives them privileged access to participants and a context that they also wish to study. Alternatively, the researcher may explicitly set out to learn the role, gaining an understanding of the work and of the roles of technology in that work through both learning and performing the role.

Action research (Reason and Bradbury, 2001; Rogers, 2012; Kock, 2013) involves actively intervening in the situation, introducing a new technology or a new method, and studying in detail the effect of the intervention. It has been described as doing experiments in the field. It has been proposed as a method for mobile HCI (Kjeldskov and Graham, 2003) and community-based projects (Hayes, 2011). It is generally good practice in action research to determine important measures of change (e.g., based on participant attitudes, times to perform tasks or measures of the quality of the work) and to gather information on those measures before and after the intervention (e.g., through a survey). This quantitative data can then be related to the qualitative data that is gathered through the core of the action research project (see discussion of mixed methods later in this chapter). As with many other approaches, completing multiple cycles of action research in the same, or related, study settings can increase confidence in the validity of the findings (Kock, 2013).

Both participant observation and action research require the researcher to actively gather data (through interviews and observation) while also reflecting on their role within the study setting, and on the nature and effects of their intervention. It is essential for the researcher to maintain good field notes, and often a reflective diary.

## 6.2.6    GROUNDED THEORY

As noted above, the term "Grounded Theory" (GT) is widely used in HCI as a label for any method that involves systematic coding of data, regardless of the details of the study design. This might be a Thematic Analysis, or a comparatively unstructured and superficial analysis. We are using the term in a narrower sense that is closer to its origins, to capture some of the important features of this approach.

GT is not a theory, but an approach to theory development at its most developed level, i.e., a full conceptual system that is grounded in data. Alternative outputs, at lower levels of development, include: basic taxonomy development, focused conceptual development and cycles of interpretation (Pidgeon and Henwood, 1996). There are several accounts of GT and how to apply it, including Glaser and Strauss (2009); Corbin and Strauss (2015); Charmaz (2014); Adams et al. (2008) and Lazar et al. (2010). Grbich (2013) identifies three main versions of GT, which she refers to as Straussian (involving a detailed, prescriptive three-stage coding process), Glaserian (involving a less detailed and prescriptive coding process but more emphasis on shifting between levels of analysis to relate the details to the big picture), and Charmaz's (which has a stronger interpretivist emphasis). Which approach is appropriate depends partly on the problem your study is addressing and partly on you and what resonates with the way you think.

There is widespread agreement among those who describe how to apply GT that it should involve:

- **interleaving between data gathering and analysis:** where findings from one interview or observation are used to guide subsequent ones;

- **avoiding bringing pre-conceived expectations of what might be found:** although Glaser and Strauss disagree about the use of existing literature, all approaches warn against forcing findings to fit pre-existing theory or existing literature;

- **theoretical sampling:** recruiting participants who are likely to build on and enhance the theory that is emerging from data collection and analysis, rather than fixing a sample from the outset, e.g., based on particular demographics; and

- theory constructed from data through a process of **constant comparative analysis:** where findings are constantly compared with each other to spot patterns and generate new insights.

Comparing Grounded Theory (GT) with Thematic Analysis (TA) (Chapter 5), we find commonalities, particularly in the value given to iteration in analysis, to the centrality of data and to the development of explanatory narratives and themes. However, there are also important points of contrast. Firstly, TA seems more open to the analysis being informed by prior literature and established theory from the outset, although the aim should never be to just confirm or accept established theory without question. In GT, data drives the analysis rather than previous theory and literature, though findings are often compared to existing work. Secondly, data gathering and analysis should be interleaved in GT. Corbin and Strauss (2015) refer to this as a "cyclic process" of data gathering and analysis. In contrast, TA works with an existing dataset. Therefore while GT is used for both data analysis *and* collection, TA is an approach to analysis. Further, in GT, recruitment of participants should be "theoretical," i.e., specifically aiming to develop the theory. The interviews, observations, focus groups, etc., should be tailored to also develop the emerging theory further, until "theoretical saturation" is reached. As explained previously, this is where further data gathering and analysis does not help to develop the theory further.

This process is sketched in Figure 6.3, where the funnel "wine glass" represents the breadth and depth of the evolving theory, while the spiral represents the iterative process of recruitment, data gathering and analysis. Each circuit around the "wine glass" represents a single stage of recruitment, data gathering and analysis. As data analysis proceeds, the theory becomes more focused (based on theoretical sampling of participants and more focused data gathering and analysis), and correspondingly deeper and better evidenced. It is difficult to anticipate at the outset exactly how the theory will develop. Indeed, there may be occasions (in larger studies) where an important theme is intentionally set aside part-way through the study, then picked up and developed later, possibly resulting in a second "stem" on the "wine glass."

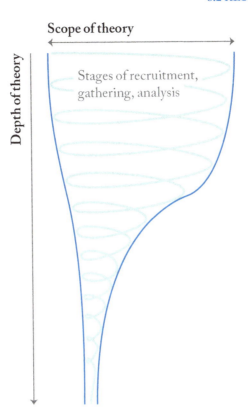

**Figure 6.3:** A simplified view of how Grounded Theory recruitment, data gathering and analysis may progress. The scope of the theory generated starts off broad, narrowing as we learn more.

Furniss et al. (2011a) present a reflective account of our experiences of applying GT in an HCI context, which was to examine why practitioners use the user evaluation methods that they do. The account focuses particularly on pragmatic "lessons learnt." These include practical issues such as managing time and the challenges of recruiting participants, and also theoretical issues such as reflecting on the role of existing theory and the background of the analyst in informing the findings. There are both potential benefits and drawbacks to already having a detailed understanding of existing theory in the area before conducting a GT study. Benefits include better understanding the area of study before the research begins, avoiding rediscovery of theories or principles that are, in fact, already widely recognised, and being more readily able to spot what is new or original in your findings. Drawbacks include the possibility of unwittingly steering the research in the direction of existing theory when an alternative direction might have yielded more interesting or novel findings, and the possibility of unintentionally shoehorning findings into existing theory because the existing theory is fresh in your mind (see Makri et al., 2011 for a discussion on shoehorning during data analysis). Furniss et al. (2011a) also explore using existing theory as a lens on more traditional GT analyses. We revisit the challenge of how to relate findings to existing theory and literature in Chapter 7.

## 6.3    MIXED METHODS AND STAGED APPROACHES

It can often be valuable to combine methods to gain a richer understanding of the situation. This may involve gathering both qualitative and quantitative data within one study, or running separate, complementary studies. An example of the first might be gathering quantitative data on user interaction metrics (such as number of pages viewed) while also gathering qualitative data through a think-aloud study. An example of the second might be conducting interviews to probe data from diary studies. In this section, we discuss the approach of intentionally designing a study in multiple phases, exploiting the value of intermediate review and of the use of complementary approaches.

One approach—probably the simplest approach to multi-stage studies—is simply to plan data gathering and analysis in multiple phases. This has some of the benefits of a GT study design but is often quicker to perform (and hence more feasible when time is tight, as in most MSc projects). In this approach, data gathering is planned in two or more phases, with in-depth analysis after the first phase in order to focus the data gathering in the second phase. For example, Rajkomar (Rajkomar et al., 2015) visited his first five participants at their homes for detailed observations and interviews on two or three occasions each, then did a preliminary round of data analysis, constructing DCog models and identifying safety strategies for those participants. He reviewed which kinds of observations and lines of questioning were most productive for the analysis, and streamlined the data gathering plan so that he only had to visit each subsequent participant (a further 14) once each; this was less disruptive for participants as well as being a more effective use of his time.

Another approach is to use complementary methods of data gathering to build a richer picture of the situation. As discussed earlier, observations give a more reliable account of 'what is' or "what is done" while interviews give greater insight into why things are done or people's perceptions and experiences of particular technologies. Approaches such as Contextual Inquiry intentionally combine these to give a richer overall understanding of the situation and of technology practices and needs. It is also often useful to complement semi-structured qualitative studies with quantitative ones; for example, conducting surveys to see how far findings from a small set of interviews or observations generalise across the user population of interest, or conversely using interviews and observations to understand particular survey findings in more detail (e.g., surprising findings). Here different methods can complement and build on each other's findings.

Different methods can also provide coverage in breadth and depth, where one method on its own might leave gaps. For example, where it is not feasible to observe people—whether because the technology is used infrequently or sporadically or because it is not used in a fixed location (e.g., mobile and ubiquitous technologies)—interviews can again give insights into people's perceptions and experiences. A complementary form of data gathering such as diary studies or system log analyses can provide better evidence on people's practices. For example, as noted earlier, Kamsin et al. (2012) complemented their interview study of 26 participants with a video diary study; they asked 7 people to keep a video diary documenting how they managed to-do items over a period of 1–3 weeks. One important to-do management strategy that hardly featured in the interviews, but was prominent in the video diaries, was that a lot of to-do items arrive by email but most email tools are poor at managing to-do items.

Mixing methods can sometimes result in unintended effects. In particular, keeping a diary can, in some situations, change the nature of the study significantly. For example, Laurie and Blandford (2016) were studying people's adoption and use of a mindfulness app, but wanted that use to be as naturalistic as possible. To test whether keeping a diary was likely to have a significant impact on people's engagement with the app, as well as to better understand the experience of using the app, Laurie first completed an autoethnography (as described above). He used the app himself for 30 days and maintained a diary of his experiences. This complementary study served three purposes. Firstly, it gave direct insight into the experience of using the app (being a source of data in its own right). Secondly, it helped identify many areas of inquiry for interviews that he would not have considered previously. Further, it confirmed his suspicion that the act of keeping a reflexive diary changed the experience of using the app substantively, so the main user study was designed to gather data just through initial and debriefing interviews.

When applying mixed methods, such as in these examples, some researchers choose to merge all the data into one set for analysis. While this may have some benefits in terms of identifying key themes that emerge through multiple data gathering methods, it also sacrifices on detail. At least initially, it is more prudent to analyse each dataset as it is acquired, making it clear what the purpose and outcome of each phase of data gathering and analysis was, and how each built on earlier phases. It is always possible to do a subsequent re-analysis of the combined dataset. It is very difficult to go the other way, and unpack what insights were derived from each data gathering approach and how each study contributed to the overall understanding once datasets have been merged.

Figure 6.4: It is important to have a plan and a direction, but plans must be updated and adapted when responding to the situation.

## 6.4    RESPONDING TO THE SITUATION

Where research is truly exploratory, the situation is likely to shape the study greatly. In such studies it is impossible to plan all the details of the study ahead of time and get them all right. The details have to evolve as understanding of the context and subject matter matures. This evolution is made explicit in the processes and ethos of GT, but can apply to other SSQSs that do not follow all the principles of GT.

As should already be apparent, there are many connections and interdependencies between considerations when designing, conducting and reporting SSQSs, and these phases of work are not generally distinct. Through engaging with the study setting, the researcher learns more about what is possible in terms of data gathering, and more about the nuances of the research question, so the purpose of the study may change, at least in subtle ways, as understanding evolves. Unlike most quantitative studies, which can conveniently be treated as starting with a hypothesis and finishing with a conclusion (even if the truth is not quite that simple), many SSQSs are effectively journeys, in which the researcher travels alongside the participants, making discoveries that are shared through the reporting of the study. So the focus for data gathering and analysis may change, shaped by current understanding, as the study proceeds. Furthermore, as discussed in earlier sections, the study is shaped by the individuals (researchers and participants) engaged in it, by any extant theory that is exploited in the study, by resources and constraints and by ethical considerations.

Earlier (Figure 2.3) we presented a simplified view of the research process for a qualitative study. Figure 6.5 shows a process that is closer to reality, with feedback and evolution in all stages as a study progresses, still shaped by the same external factors. Data gathering and analysis may be closely or loosely coupled. Early analysis may lead to revisions in the purpose of the study. The process of reporting often leads to new understanding of the problem. Or, indeed, the reporting of findings from a study may lead to new questions that shape the purposes of future studies. The overall purpose may be broken down into sub-questions that are best addressed through complementary studies involving different data gathering and analysis methods. These studies may be reported singly or together. Described in this way, the process can appear complicated and daunting. But the inter-relationships between the different parts of the process actually provide opportunity for reflection and clarification, which can improve the overall quality of the research. It is also unusual for the study to change beyond recognition as a result of this dynamic process; the space of possibilities for refinement is usually not very great. This, thankfully, means that qualitative studies can be flexible and adaptive without being unmanageable.

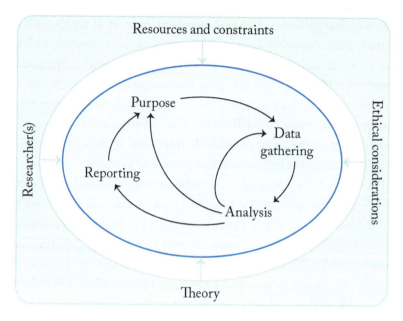

Figure 6.5: Closer to reality: qualitative research as a journey shaped by many factors.

Another factor that can have a great influence on findings is the participants. The purpose of the study will determine who are ideal or possible participants, which may relate more-or-less directly to people's likely motivations for participating. This, in turn, should shape and be shaped by the recruitment strategy, discussed in Chapter 3. Participants will shape what data gathering and validation is possible and hence the quality of data analysis, which will determine the actual outcomes of the study. These outcomes should address the purpose of the study, or may lead the research team to review and revise the purpose of the study (Figure 6.6). It is important to invest effort early in the study to make recruitment and data gathering as effective as possible for the purpose of the study.

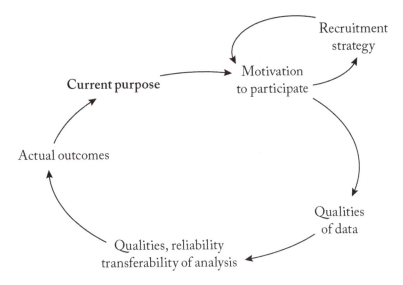

Figure 6.6: Interdependencies between the purpose of a study, recruitment of participants and outcomes (which should match the purpose).

In some situations, data gathering and analysis are treated as being semi-independent from each other, with analysis following data gathering. In other situations, the two are interleaved—whether in the rich way advocated in GT, or by interleaving stages of data gathering and analysis as a study proceeds—e.g., as the theoretical focus develops, or as different data gathering methods are applied to address the problem from different angles. This can of course also be done over multiple studies that build on each other. It is helpful to monitor progress as the study proceeds, and to select data gathering and analysis methods to give the best possible data and outcome.

## 6.5    SUMMARY AND CHECKLIST: STUDY SHAPING ISSUES

Studies are shaped by a number of factors, including the purpose and style of the study, resources and constraints, ethical considerations and existing theory. They are also often shaped by the people involved in them—the researcher and participants. Although it can feel unnerving to allow your study to be shaped by factors not entirely within your control, being flexible and dynamic in your approach to being shaped can result in insightful and potentially surprising findings.

Checklist E summarises some of the study shaping issues that need to be considered early on and throughout the study. Considering these issues will allow you to develop approaches for consciously shaping your research and for dealing with situations when your research is shaped outside of your direct control.

| Checklist E: Study shaping issues | |
|---|---|
| **Purpose and approach** | How will the purpose of the study shape data collection and analysis? How structured or exploratory is the study? Will the research involve multiple complementary approaches? Will the chosen approach(es) allow for reflection on and revision of the study's purpose? |
| **Style of study** | Where will the study be situated across the continuum of styles of qualitative study? What approach is appropriate for this particular study? What makes the approach chosen particularly appropriate? |
| **Researcher** | Will the researcher's background and biases shape the study? If so, how? Will multiple researchers collect or analyse the data? Why/why not? |
| **Participants** | How will the recruitment strategy maximise the potential for suitable participants? What impact does participant choice and availability have on data gathering? What relationship is there between researcher and participants, and how will that shape the study? |
| **Theory** | Will the study make use of existing theory (e.g., to test, extend or enrich it)? If yes, how will confirmation bias be avoided? Will the findings be discussed in relation to previous related work? If so, when will the researcher become familiar with this work? |

# CHAPTER 7

# Reporting

## *CREATING THE FINAL CUT*

The final step is to deliver the finished product. In the latter stages of film-making a rough cut is turned into a final cut as it is refined by the editor, director and producer. Perhaps even more so, the writing up of a qualitative study is usually an ongoing process that involves cycles of iteration. Early drafts of a dissertation, paper or report are often effectively refinements of the analysis.

As with any writing, the reporting of a study has to be appropriate to the audience. If the study has been commissioned to deliver findings rapidly as part of a commercial development process, the reporting should be appropriately succinct and focused, whereas if it is part of a Master's or Ph.D. dissertation or another large academic project, the reporting is more likely to focus on novel contribution to knowledge and relationship to theory and previous literature.

The most important advice on writing is to start early and write often. Committing thoughts to writing forces you to articulate your thinking, which reciprocally can impact thinking. Ask others such as your dissertation supervisors or colleagues for feedback. For qualitative studies, feedback is not only important for improving presentation quality, but for testing the quality of the argumentation and evidence. Feedback can also help you check whether you are writing clearly and at an appropriate level of detail to enable others to assess the quality of the research.

When writing up scientific papers, including quantitative HCI studies, there are established reporting structures that are widely conformed to: aims, background, method, results, discussion and conclusion. Many, but not all, qualitative HCI studies follow this structure. There is no single correct approach to structuring write-ups of qualitative studies. For example, Wolcott (2009) argues that only essential background material should be included as part of the introduction, and that other related work should be introduced as needed through the narrative. Sometimes results and discussion are integrated into one section. Often, when you discover relevant literature partway and at the end of a study, a decision must be made about whether to refer to this in the background section (as if you knew about it beforehand) or only in the discussion section. If the final understanding and all the literature that relates to that understanding is presented up-front, the findings can seem underwhelming even though they were not anticipated at the beginning. Instead, it can be valuable to take the reader through highlights of the journey that the researcher has travelled so that the reader is exposed to some of the delight of discovery that the research team experienced, assuming that the researchers started from a sensible place.

For example, as discussed above, one MSc student started with the purpose of understanding how underground train controllers use technology and work together, with the intention of conducting DCog analyses of different control rooms to understand variability in design and practices. As the study progressed, it became clear that the commonalities between them were much greater than the contrasts, and that a more interesting question was how the culture and use of technology has evolved to maintain safety. We decided to focus the background section of the subsequent paper (Smith et al., 2009) on principles of train control, based on both literature and our early data gathering, then to contextualise our findings in terms of the literature on resilience (e.g., Rochlin, 1999) and serious games (e.g., Garris et al., 2002).

In quantitative research, the researcher's understanding of the problem is unlikely to change much during a study, unless the hypothesis is poorly founded or the method inadequately planned or executed. In contrast, in an SSQS the researcher is likely to learn a lot about the problem, and to see it in different ways as understanding matures (e.g., Furniss et al., 2011a). For example, a researcher who is doing a situated study of technology use in an unfamiliar environment is learning about the study context, beyond what can be read in published material about it, while doing the study. Yet the details of the context are part of the background to the research, and not usually research findings. The boundaries between data analysis, method and results, between results and discussion and between discussion and conclusions can seem just as blurred, particularly as understanding deepens through iterations of analysis. With some well-planned and executed quantitative HCI studies, it is possible to write up much if not all of the aims, background and method sections before gathering any data. This is very difficult, if not impossible, to do with qualitative studies. How to frame a contribution from a qualitative study might only be apparent after the analysis, and there may be different framings for different audiences, so the whole endeavour is much more flexible.

Understanding develops as further data is gathered (e.g., Charmaz, 2014) and as new theoretical perspectives are encountered as ways of making sense of the data (e.g., Furniss et al., 2011a). Braun and Clarke (2006, p. 80) note that an "account of themes 'emerging' or being 'discovered' is a passive account of the process of analysis, and it denies the active role the researcher always plays in identifying patterns/themes." This highlights the fact that there are alternative ways of reporting, depending on the role(s) that the researcher has played in the research process. Bringing the researcher into the narrative makes explicit their role, which may make the research findings seem less objective or authoritative than a more "distanced" account. Within HCI, the highly personalised account is rare, as it can undermine the expectation that the account is objective to inform design. Yet there may be times, such as when delivering rich accounts of user experience to help designers put themselves in the users' shoes, when such a personalised account is more effective and conveys a higher level of integrity than a depersonalised one.

Figure 7.1: Not all the data can be presented and so it must be selected to support the narrative but in a way that does not introduce distortions and respects the participants.

It is important to report in a way that respects participants (Lipson, 1997). If they read the write-up, how are participants likely to feel about the reporting? For example, if a study reports errors that people make with technology then it needs to be done in a way that does not make participants feel either stupid or vulnerable. It is good practice to give participants the opportunity not only to check over their transcripts but also the reporting, where possible. It is also important to be open, thorough and accurate in your reporting. Integrity is an essential characteristic of a good qualitative researcher; as qualitative data and data analysis is more subjective than quantitative research, it is especially important for researchers to be open, honest, transparent, accurate and thorough when reporting qualitative research. However, do not report findings in such fine-grained detail that it violates participant confidentiality, or that the reader gets bored and cannot discern important information from trivial details. It is important to balance providing enough detail to support scrutiny and accountability but not so much that it makes the work difficult to read or understand.

Qualitative HCI studies are generally reported with a scientific structure as outlined above. But there may be times where you will want to vary that structure to make the research clearer or more engaging. If you choose to write in an unconventional way, make sure you are bending the rules for good reasons. What matters most is that the account:

- has a clear **purpose** and focuses on that purpose;

- presents **essential information**, such as what was actually done (rather than textbook accounts of methods), while respecting participants and their confidentiality;

- addresses the **intended audience** (whether practitioners, other HCI researchers or specialists in the domain of the study);

- is related well to relevant **prior work**, so that it is clear what is novel about this study;

- presents findings at an **appropriate level of detail**/abstraction so that the novel contribution and the extent to which the findings generalise to other settings are clear;

- communicates clearly how exactly the study is **novel** and what new knowledge it contributes;

- is **grounded in the data**; that data is often interleaved with the narrative flow in the Results section of the paper, or sometimes kept separate (e.g., in tabular form) to make the narrative flow smoother; and

- is **coherent** as a narrative.

As noted above, it is almost impossible to get writing right the first time, and an iterative process of drafting, getting feedback from others, re-reading the draft critically (preferably after a break, to gain some distance from it) and re-drafting is essential. It is also important to know when to stop, though, because perfection is unachievable!

It is also worth considering whether there are multiple audiences or angles from the same study, to be written up separately. This not only allows researchers to write multiple complementary papers based on the same data, getting several write-ups almost for the price of one, but also allows each paper to have a distinct focus. Therefore if your report seems to have several broad themes or lots of potential audiences, then maybe it should be written up as two or three papers. If you decide to write multiple reports, take care to avoid self-plagiarism by making sure that multiple reports address different questions within the overall study purpose. An informal test of self-plagiarism is whether each paper can cite the other and be clearly different. Reporting multiple angles separately can be particularly advantageous when each paper needs to be fitted within a tight word or page limit. Tight constraints can, in practice, be very helpful for communicating effectively as it forces the author to think about what really matters in the narrative, to omit spurious information and to write succinctly. However, writing well takes time: Pascal is widely credited with the apology that "I would have written a shorter letter, but I did not have the time."

One tip is to try to find a published paper that reports the type of study that you have done. You can then use this paper as an exemplar to model your own write-up on. The most effective exemplars can be papers that follow your methodology and are already published in the journal or conference that you are targeting. This should give you an idea about their expectations in terms of style, brevity, clarity and how the authors have balanced the proportions of different sections to fit within the page limit. For example, we often recommend that students look at Winkelman et al. (2005) as a clear and succinct GT write-up that reports four themes.

## 7.1    COMMUNICATING QUALITY THROUGH REPORTING

We have left the topic of quality until the end (Chapter 8) because it is associated with all aspects of research, but it is particularly important to communicate the quality of your study through the way you report it. While we would all like others to think that our study is faultless, this is unlikely to be true. It is more useful for both you and your readers if you can clearly communicate both the strengths and the limitations of your work in the write-up.

The quality of studies varies for many reasons, often linked to what is possible with the available resources, the experience and expertise of the researcher(s), the time available or the ease of recruiting an appropriate group of participants. The findings should be reported in a way that makes it possible for the reader to assess the quality of the research. The reader should be able to answer questions such as:

- What **confidence** do I have in the results and conclusions of this study? What is the evidence to support my judgement?

- What can I **learn** from this study? Relative to what was known before, what is novel?

- How can I **build** on this study?—whether on the methods, the findings or gaps in knowledge that it has exposed.

Figure 7.2 summarises questions that your reader should be asking themselves about your work, and which you should be aiming to address in your writing.

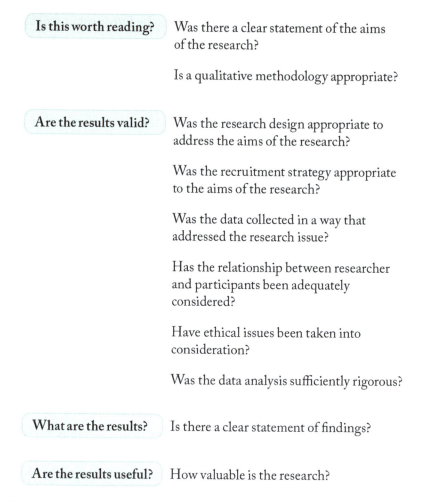

Is this worth reading?    Was there a clear statement of the aims of the research?

Is a qualitative methodology appropriate?

Are the results valid?    Was the research design appropriate to address the aims of the research?

Was the recruitment strategy appropriate to the aims of the research?

Was the data collected in a way that addressed the research issue?

Has the relationship between researcher and participants been adequately considered?

Have ethical issues been taken into consideration?

Was the data analysis sufficiently rigorous?

What are the results?    Is there a clear statement of findings?

Are the results useful?    How valuable is the research?

Figure 7.2: Appraisal questions for a qualitative study (based on CASP, 2013).

## 7.2    SUMMARY AND CHECKLIST: REPORTING A STUDY

It is important to carefully consider how best to report your qualitative HCI study. Clarity, transparency and detail (but not overwhelming amounts of detail) are important. So is ensuring that your write-up makes it clear what is novel and important in your findings. While there is no single right way of reporting a qualitative HCI study, most write-ups follow regular scientific paper conventions. But it is important to know when and how to break these conventions for the sake of producing a clearer, more engaging narrative.

Checklist F summarises issues that need to be considered in reporting a study.

| Checklist F: Reporting a qualitative HCI study | |
|---|---|
| **Purpose** | What was the original purpose of the study and did the purpose change? If so, why and how?<br>What are the novel and important findings? Why should they matter to the reader? |
| **Resources and constraints** | Were there any novel features of the way resources were used (e.g., new technology probes or innovative use of social media)?<br>Did the availability of resources (e.g., time) limit what was possible in important ways?<br>Are there attributes of the research team that will have influenced the study in important ways?<br>What role(s) did the researcher(s) play in the study setting?<br>How did the relationship that was established with each participant influence the data that was gathered (if it is possible to tell)?<br>Who did you work with, and what was their influence (e.g., in terms of helping to refine research questions or recruit participants)?<br>How were participants recruited in practice? Were there compromises that needed to be made, and what is the likely impact of this on the quality, reliability or generalisability of findings?<br>What roles did researcher(s) and participant(s) take in the study?<br>Did the location(s) in which the study took place, or any interventions, influence outcomes in any important ways?<br>How, if at all, did established theory shape the study? How do the findings relate to established theory? |
| **Ethical considerations** | Did ethical considerations shape the study in important ways? If so, how?<br>Does the reporting respect the participants? |
| **Techniques for data gathering** | How was data gathered in practice? How did data gathering change over the course of the study (if at all)?<br>How were participants instructed (e.g., for a think-aloud study)?<br>How were data gathering and analysis interleaved (if at all)? How did early analysis shape later data gathering? |
| **Analysis of data** | How was data analysed in practice? How iterative and reflexive was the analysis process?<br>How was data validated in practice? See Chapter 8. |
| **Reporting** | What is novel? What is important? What is the evidence to support the claims being made? |

# CHAPTER 8

# Ensuring Quality in Qualitative Research

## *CRITICS AND REVIEWS*

Once a film is ready for release, it will usually be subject to critical review. What the critics will see and assess is the finished product. But of course, the quality of that product will depend on the quality of the work of the entire film team (director, editor, film crew, etc.). It is very difficult to deliver a high quality product if you do not have a high quality process. The same is true of qualitative studies. In this chapter, we review quality from the perspectives of both the research team and reviewers of the research.

Achieving and communicating quality can be challenging for SSQSs, where there is no hypothesis, the themes that emerge from the data may be very different from what the researcher expected, and the individual personalities of researchers and participants and their situations can have a big influence over the progress of the study and the findings.

## 8.1    STARTING WITH THE BASICS

People who do not appreciate qualitative approaches can subscribe to any of the following views: that it is easy, wishy washy, not generalisable, biased, too subjective, lacking in appropriate criteria to judge its quality, and that it works within the realms of anecdotes rather than science. This is not an exhaustive list and in the worst cases people may subscribe to all of these and more. They may perceive qualitative researchers as saying derivations of, "I had a chat with a few people and after thinking about it a bit I reckon the system is fairly good." It is worth deconstructing this view and remembering some of the basics of qualitative research that we have covered in previous chapters and will cover in this chapter.

- **"I had a chat…"**—this refers to the data gathering technique which should be detailed and systematic. In Chapter 4, we outlined many of the methods that are available for engaging with rich qualitative material and phenomena in different ways.

- **"...with a few people..."**—this refers to the sampling technique and recruitment strategy. In Chapter 3, we reviewed types of sampling and recruitment for different scenarios, which will have a bearing on the data and the resultant findings.

- **"...and after thinking about it..."**—this refers to the type of analysis which can range in depth depending on the purpose of the research, the method and data and resources and constraints. In Chater 5, we reviewed different coding processes and the QDA tools that can support these processes.

- **"...a bit..."**—this refers to the level of rigour in the analysis. In Chater 5 we indicated how hours of interviews quickly translates to many days of analysis.

- **"...I reckon..."**—this is the confidence you have in your results which is tied to the measures of validity you have employed. We review different techniques for external validation in this chapter.

- **"...the system is fairly good."**—this refers to the claims made from the research. We review how these should be transferable and useful, as well as rigorous and creative, in this chapter.

In disciplines such as healthcare, there is a persistent view that randomised controlled trials are the "gold standard" that defines criteria for quality in research (Concato et al., 2000). Thankfully, the field of HCI has acknowledged that research can demonstrate quality in several ways, and that these ways are likely to differ across qualitative and quantitative research. However, there has been less recognition so far that quality criteria are also likely to differ across traditions of qualitative research. This has resulted in a tendency to dismiss some forms of qualitative research as lacking rigour. While this is true of some studies, it often seems to be due to limited understanding of the culture, principles and processes of qualitative research. Over time, a more widespread understanding of different types and traditions of qualitative HCI research will address this issue.

## 8.2    BUILDING QUALITY INTO THE PROCESS

One of the challenges for qualitative researchers in HCI is that those who are not familiar with the various styles of qualitative research have little idea of how to assess the quality of qualitative research. Many reviewers adopt a particular stance (e.g., positivist or interpretivist), and immediately criticise research that does not conform to the expected paradigm. Arguably, on the one hand it is incumbent on the authors of a qualitative paper to present their approach and the rationale for it clearly, while on the other hand the reviewer has a responsibility to have appropriate expertise or an open mind, or to decline to review.

The following are criteria that have been identified by leading authors and committees who have considered the question of what constitutes quality in qualitative research.

**Appropriateness of methods:** This concerns the overall coherence of the study. Given the purpose of the study, were the best possible data gathered from suitable participants, in relevant study settings, using appropriate data gathering techniques? Was the data analysis approach suitable?

**Sensitivity to context:** Yardley (2000) emphasises the importance of taking account of previous relevant research, as well as listening deeply to participants' perspectives and being sensitive to ethical considerations. Klein and Myers (1999) emphasise the importance of enabling the reader to fully comprehend the context of the research.

**Commitment and rigour:** How well does the research engage with the topic and with participants? How systematic and thorough was the data analysis?

**Transparency and coherence:** Yardley (2000) notes the importance of making it clear how data was analysed and conclusions drawn. Similarly, Henwood and Pidgeon (1992) advocate keeping close to the data so that the link between data and conclusions is clear, and maintaining a "paper trail" that is open to external audit to expose the layers of analysis.

**Impact and importance:** Yardley (2000) emphasises the importance of articulating clearly both the theoretical and practical significance of findings. In HCI studies, this may, but does not necessarily, include "implications for design" (Dourish, 2006). It may also include insight that helps to understand work, interaction or experience with technology in a new way. Klein and Myers (1999) argue that importance is achieved through abstraction and generalisation, i.e., relating the particulars of the study to general principles.

**Generalisability:** According to Lewis and Ritchie (2003), generalisability can be split into theoretical and empirical generalisability. Theoretical generalisability is the extent to which the theory and concepts generated from the study apply to existing theory and concepts. For example, as discussed in Chapter 6, we made sense of nurses' interactions with computer systems in terms of theory from Communities of Practice (Adams et al., 2005). Empirical generalisability is the extent to which the findings from one study apply to other contexts. For example, the patterns of behaviour displayed by nurses might also apply to radiographers and physiotherapists. By first abstracting the results up to broader theory (vertically), the more abstract theory would have wider applicability to different contexts (horizontally).

**Transferability:** While generalisability is determined by researchers, through further research, transferability is determined by readers of the research. It is the extent to which the findings relate to the reader's own experiences. To facilitate transferability, Henwood and Pidgeon (1992) suggest that researchers should report on the contextual aspects of the study. This is so that the reader is equipped to assess the sphere of relevance of the findings. Transferability and generalisability are closely linked; findings that can be applied to a variety of different study contexts are likely to be more readily applied by readers to their own situations. Indeed, Lewis and Ritchie (2003) equate transferability with empirical generalisability.

**Reflexivity:** Reflexivity involves the researcher asking themselves thoughtful questions about their own influence on their findings and research. This is different from reflecting on research that involves the researcher asking themselves thoughtful questions about their data collection and analysis. Adams et al. (2008) describe two types of reflexivity: personal and epistemological reflexivity. Personal reflexivity involves the researcher asking themselves how their background, sex, interests, expertise, experiences and beliefs are shaping (and potentially biasing) the research. Epistemological reflexivity involves the researcher asking themselves how their approach, philosophy and theoretical biases are shaping (and potentially biasing) the research.

Figure 8.1: Reflexivity is not just about reflecting on the methods for data collection and analysis, but thinking about how one's background, biases and identity may have impacted the findings for better or for worse.

**Theoretical sampling and negative case analysis:** Henwood and Pidgeon (1992) suggest that actively looking for cases in the data that do not fit emerging theoretical findings helps to challenge assumptions and refine the emerging theory. They argue that this is closely related to constant comparison—a method advocated within the GT tradition for continually comparing new with existing findings. As well as being sensitive to contradictory evidence, Klein and Myers (1999) note the importance of being open to multiple interpretations (e.g., contradictory views of the same situation from different participants). Opposing views may result in multiple narratives that acknowledge the different viewpoints.

**Suspicion and scepticism:** Klein and Myers (1999) also argue that the analyst should be sensitive to possible systematic distortions in qualitative data. These may stem from the way participants were recruited, or shaped by people's motivations for participating in the study. Corbin and Strauss (2015) suggest remaining skeptical about emerging findings, regularly checking assumptions about whether what we think we are finding is actually present in the data.

**Iterating between details and big picture:** A high-quality qualitative narrative is likely to be detailed but also provide the reader with an understanding of the whole—helping them to "see the wood from the trees." Without enough detail, the narrative is likely to be unconvincing or superficial. Without some abstraction from the detail, the narrative is likely to be difficult to contextualise, impacting transferability. To create a strong narrative, the researcher must cycle between understanding the details of the research and the big picture, during data analysis. Corbin and Strauss (2015) suggest regularly stepping back from the research "to ask what is going on here in an abstract sense" (p. 21).

**Creativity:** Many of the quality criteria discussed above emphasise a rigorous and systematic approach to planning and conducting qualitative research. But creativity is also an essential attribute of high-quality research. Creativity involves having ideas that are both original and useful (Byron, 2013). Research should be aiming to make an original contribution to knowledge—e.g., by reporting findings that enhance or question previous research, by creating new theory or challenging or enriching existing theory or by coming up with novel approaches or designs. That contribution to knowledge should generally be useful within and beyond academia—e.g., to HCI researchers, researchers from the study domain, HCI practitioners, users and policymakers. Creative thinking can be useful at all stages of research, from coming up with research aims or questions that have not been examined before, to identifying ways of building on previous research, pioneering new approaches to data collection and analysis and even to reporting findings. For example, the conventional way of feeding findings from observations of information interaction behaviour into design is to make design suggestions for better supporting the observed behaviour (which we did in Makri et. al., 2008a); we also created two new user evaluation methods underpinned by our theory (Makri et al., 2008b) so that HCI designers could use our findings to assess how well existing interactive systems support this behaviour. We also reported participants' memorable examples of coming across information serendipitously (Makri and Blandford, 2012; Makri et al., 2014) more creatively, as "serendipity stories" that were written in the first person and based closely on participants' accounts. We even asked an artist to illustrate some of the stories and a voice actor to narrate them, sharing the videos on YouTube and using them in presentations (see Figure 8.2).

Figure 8.2: Sample from the "Daily Dose of Tubeworms" artwork. Created by Johanna Basford, artistic concept by Mel Woods (https://www.youtube.com/watch?v=Ct00fVYum8Y).

Most of these criteria for quality depend on the researcher conducting high quality data gathering, analysing rigorously and reporting with integrity, and presenting the process with clarity and transparency. This maximises the potential for the research to be useful to others. Creativity is also, however, extremely important; in order for research to be useful it should deliver original insights that allow the reader to think about the research area in new ways. Keeping in mind how other people will find your work both useful and insightful is essential.

## 8.3    EXTERNAL VALIDATION: INTER-RATER RELIABILITY, TRIANGULATION AND RESPONDENT VALIDATION

There are various approaches that provide external validation of an analysis, which may be appropriate and feasible under some circumstances. These include using multiple coders, triangulation of data sources and respondent validation. These methods are typically built into the study design.

For positivist studies, the use of multiple coders is widely advocated. Miles and Huberman (1994, p. 11) emphasise the importance of conclusions being verified, whether by reference back to field notes, achieving "intersubjective consensus" through discussion with colleagues, or replicating findings in another dataset. They focus on the agreement of codes between multiple analysts—an approach that can be validated through measures of inter-rater reliability if coding is done independently. Pennathur et al. (2013) worked in a similar tradition, developing an approach to analysis that involved achieving group consensus for reconciling discrepancies between coders rather than computing inter-rater reliability. This required that a set of codes had been previously agreed on; in their case, these were based on the Systems Engineering Initiative for Patient Safety (SEIPS) model (Carayon et al., 2006)—i.e., a particular theoretical perspective.

Having multiple independent coders of data and checking inter-rater reliability is appropriate for studies where codes and their meanings have been agreed on and where the analysis and reporting relies heavily on those codes. It is not an appropriate way to validate a rich interpretive analysis, as different coders are likely to interpret the data in different (but hopefully complementary) ways. These types of studies are best validated internally, through regular assumption checking and constant comparison.

Another widely used approach is respondent validation, or member checking, in which study participants are invited to review the study findings to validate the researcher's interpretation of the data. A variant on this is to have other representatives of the same group (people "like" the participants) review the findings. While some (e.g., Lincoln and Guba, 1985) regard this as a strong check, others (e.g., Mays and Pope, 2000) highlight weaknesses in the approach, including dealing with discrepancies in the responses of participants (which effectively represent new data to be analysed) and managing the different priorities and focuses of participants and researchers. Rather than conducting standard respondent validation, Henwood and Pidgeon (1992) suggest that negotiating interpretations with participants may sometimes be an effective approach to validating interpretations.

In other situations, including many interpretivist studies, it is possible to employ triangulation, which involves comparing multiple data sources or different methods of gathering data to corroborate findings. Mackay and Fayard (1997) argue that triangulation is particularly valuable in HCI. Guion (2002) lists four different approaches to triangulation.

1. **Data triangulation:** data is obtained from multiple sources and compared. These sources may be, for example, different participant groups that are each likely to provide insights into the research problem. This helps with assessing the generalisability of findings; if findings are corroborated across sources, they are more likely to be generalisable.

2. **Investigator triangulation:** different researchers collect and interpret the data; this is similar to the use of multiple coders as advocated by Miles and Huberman (1994). But the multiple coders are used for both data collection and analysis.

3. **Triangulation of theories:** using different theoretical frameworks as lenses on the data or findings. This has the potential to provide multiple perspectives on the findings.

4. **Methodological triangulation:** employing multiple data gathering techniques (e.g., both interviews and observations) can help to ensure the outcome is not a simple function of the way that data was gathered.

Mays and Pope (2000) propose that, rather than supporting validation directly, triangulation encourages a more reflexive analysis of the available data. Different forms of triangulation can support data validation and give greater confidence in the findings, in different ways. See the earlier discussions on using multiple methods and reflexivity in analysis.

A further, informal, check is face validity: do the findings of the study make sense? Are they credible? On its own, face validity is a very weak test, and should always be viewed with a critical eye, but the converse can be helpful: findings that lack face validity are rightly viewed with suspicion and should be investigated further.

Barbour (2001) suggests that in qualitative healthcare research, there is a tendency towards a "checklist mentality": that what she calls "technical fixes" are being requested by funders or reviewers to ensure the rigour of qualitative research, but that applying these fixes blindly and prescriptively may not actually improve the research. She highlights five such fixes: purposive sampling; Grounded Theory; multiple coding; triangulation; and respondent validation. For each, she discusses the potential benefits (reducing bias; supporting original theorising; enhancing inter-rater reliability; checking internal validity; and checking researchers' interpretations, respectively). She also highlights pragmatic limitations of each approach in practice, and argues (p. 1117) that "they can strengthen the rigour of qualitative research only if they are embedded in a broad understanding of qualitative research design and data analysis." We would add that these different checks are mutually incompatible: for example, that the positivist assumptions underlying multiple coding are inconsistent with the interpretivist stance of GT. Although we present checklists to assist researchers, we do not advocate a checklist mentality. In our experience, making sure that there is quality in the process (see previous section) gives much greater assurance of overall quality than retrospective quality checking of the outcome. Also, approaches used to ensure quality should be compatible with the overall research approach.

## 8.4   SUMMARY AND CHECKLIST: QUALITY OF QUALITATIVE RESEARCH

In qualitative HCI studies, the validity, transferability and generalisability of findings is important: if design decisions for future systems are to be based on those findings, there has to be confidence in their broader applicability, or at least an understanding of how broad their applicability is. Some confidence in generalisability can come from relating findings to established theory or by triangulating findings across different data sources; one source of confidence is that the findings from the current study are consistent with those from other studies (whether represented directly in their findings or through theory that abstracts from findings). If findings differ in interesting ways from theory or previous studies, this does not automatically imply lack of generalisability. But it does merit further discussion on how the difference can be accounted for (e.g., because of some important difference in study conditions, such as taking place in a different kind of setting or working with a different user population). Alternatively, particularly where there is no relevant prior theory or data, the findings from a qualitative study might indicate the need for further research to validate those findings.

Quality criteria such as validity, transferability and generalisability help determine how useful the research findings are to others. But usefulness also depends on the nature and breadth of insight that can be gained from them. The more insightful the findings the more valuable they are likely to be, to a broader variety of people—in and beyond academia. Therefore creativity plays an essential, but rarely discussed, role in research quality.

For reviewers of papers reporting SSQSs, the question is basic: is this paper worth publishing?; does it make a useful, original and valid contribution to knowledge and to the community? It is probably impossible to conduct a "perfect" study in any research paradigm: with more resources, it is almost always possible to do a better job. But we should strive to make our research as good as we possibly can, rather than simply try to do a "good enough" job.

In earlier chapters, we have outlined some of the dimensions on which qualitative studies vary. In this chapter we have summarised key aspects of quality in qualitative studies; methods and approaches to quality control and validation should be coherent, and appropriate to the purpose, resources and methods of the study.

Checklist G summarises some of the issues that need to be considered when reviewing the quality of a study, whether at the time of writing a research proposal or when reviewing a study that has been written up.

| Checklist G: Reviewing the quality of a SSQS | |
|---|---|
| **Purpose** | Is the purpose of the study clear? |
| | Is it an important study to conduct? |
| | Is the overall methodology well suited to the purpose of the study? |
| | Is the approach to study design and reporting appropriately creative? |
| **Resources and constraints** | Was the study well conducted given the constraints of the situation? |
| | Was the recruitment strategy appropriate? |
| | Was the role of the researcher and their relationship with participants clearly presented and appropriate? |
| **Ethical considerations** | Have all ethical considerations been addressed responsibly? |
| **Techniques for data gathering** | Was the way (or ways) data was collected appropriate to the purpose of the study? |
| | Were any novel data gathering techniques applied? |
| | Was data gathering sensitive to the context of the study? |
| **Analysis of data** | Was the data analysis rigorous? Was there sufficient iteration between details and big picture? |
| | Has the analysis been sufficiently sceptical, e.g., looking for negative cases and contradictory evidence? |
| | What evidence do you have of the validity of the findings? |
| **Reporting** | Is the reporting clear? Transparent? Thorough? |
| | What evidence is there of researcher integrity (or lack of it) and of commitment and rigour in the way the study was designed and executed? |
| | Is there transparency in the way the study was conducted and reported? |
| | Is the study design coherent? |
| | Is addressing issues of reflexivity appropriate? If so, has it been done well to explain influences on the research and findings? |
| | What are the strengths and limitations of the research and have they been reported clearly? |
| | Is the scope of the study clear? How generalisable and transferable are the findings? |
| | Are the findings original and useful? What is their significance? |

CHAPTER 9

# Conclusions and Further Resources

*LET THE CREDITS ROLL*

In this book, we have presented an overview of approaches to conducting semi-structured qualitative studies in HCI. We hope it is balanced, but we will inevitably be more familiar with and biased towards our own styles of observations and interview studies. We have not discussed in detail what you do after analysis and reporting, in terms of informing future design, deployment or training. This often involves using the insights from the qualitative study in new ways; for example, Vincent and Blandford (2015) used the outputs of qualitative studies as inputs for a set of scenarios of use for interactive medical devices. Like most other aspects of a qualitative study, this is an opportunity to be creative. But this is out of scope for this book. This book has focused mostly on what needs to happen before an SSQS (in terms of planning the study), during (in terms of data collection and analysis) and after the study (in terms of reporting and review).

## 9.1 QUALITATIVE RESEARCH: A SPACE OF POSSIBILITIES

One of the delights of qualitative studies in HCI is that they frequently deliver interesting, even surprising, findings. Qualitative HCI research can deliver rich insights that explain users' technology-related needs and usage—insights that can drive the improvement of existing technologies and the design of novel technologies. But not every qualitative research project results in design implications, nor is every project an ethnography or a GT. Every qualitative study is different, with a unique purpose and its own specific resources and constraints.

Although we have provided checklists with questions to help you reflect on aspects of qualitative data collection, analysis and reporting, we do not advocate a checklist mentality to qualitative HCI research. It is not possible to conduct a successful study by following procedures blindly and rigidly, checklist-style. A basic, superficial understanding of qualitative research is not enough, though everyone needs to start somewhere. It is necessary to build an understanding of the details to ensure that your work is high quality and results in findings that are original, insightful and useful. Instead of presenting a step-by-step guide, we have taken you behind the scenes to provide you with a better understanding of the decisions you need to make when undertaking qualitative HCI research.

Our aim in this book has been to lay out a space of possibilities and considerations for Semi-Structured Qualitative Studies in HCI. Because SSQSs are suitable for addressing a range of research questions, and because every study setting is different, there is no "one size fits all" approach: methods need to be adapted to work with the specific purpose, resources and constraints of your project. The challenge for the HCI researcher is to navigate their way through the space of possibilities, understanding the theoretical perspectives from which different authors are writing and constructing their own approach—an approach that appropriately addresses the purpose of the study, and is sympathetic to the researcher's competencies and biases and to the resources available. In Chapter 2 (Tables 2.1 and 2.2) we have outlined the purposes for which common methods and approaches are well suited; even if we have not covered every possible approach, we hope that we have equipped you to think critically about the suitability of different methods and approaches for addressing particular research questions and to be appropriately creative in your study design.

Named methods should not be used as "bumper stickers" but as a means of engaging with thoughtful questions about how you collect and analyse your data and report your findings. It is particularly important to demonstrate integrity throughout the research process, including when reporting findings. Clarity and transparency can help to demonstrate integrity. It is also important to describe your approach in enough detail to enable others to judge the quality of the work, its transferability to other settings and the implications for design and for future research and practice.

## 9.2    FURTHER RESOURCES

In preparing this book, we have drawn extensively on our own experiences of conducting and reporting qualitative studies, and those of our students. We have also consulted colleagues, textbooks, and web resources. There are also many further resources (e.g., from the social sciences) describing approaches to qualitative data analysis in detail. For example, Grbich (2013) presents over a dozen different approaches, including what she terms "classical ethnography," three variants of GT, cyber ethnography (focusing on internet use) and various approaches for analysing existing qualitative data. Flick (2009), Silverman (2013), Smith (2008) and Willig (2008) all present good general overviews of qualitative methods. There are also resources that focus specifically on data gathering, analysis or reporting. For example, Kvale and Brinkmann (2009) focus primarily on data gathering; Miles and Huberman (1994), Grbich (2013) and Braun and Clarke (2006) focus on analysis; Morse (1997), Thimbleby (2008) and Wolcott (2009) focus on reporting and other aspects of closing off a research project. You will probably find some resources that really work for you and others that do not. For example, the descriptions of TA by Braun and Clarke (2006) and by Joffe (2012) are likely to appeal to different people, or seem most applicable in different circumstances. Similarly, the different presentations and variations of GT work more or less well for different people and in different situations. You need to find what works best for you.

Figure 9.1: Integrity is important throughout the research process, from planning to data gathering and analysis. If something does not feel comfortable, explore why; e.g., it could be that some evidence is thin or you notice a source of potential bias. An open and thorough reflection on the limitations of the study and its claims can help instil integrity in the work when reporting.

## 9.3    GOING BEHIND THE SCENES

A good documentary film shares many similarities with quality research. Both must have a clear and well-defined purpose, and well-thought-out rationale for who will be taking part and why. Both require painstaking commitment and dedication when gathering data/getting footage. No matter how good the analysis/editing, the final outcome will not be interesting or useful without high quality raw material. Thoughtful, thorough analysis/editing is also essential for turning the raw material into a compelling, engaging narrative. Clarity, transparency and above all integrity are important when presenting the final outcome to ensure others rate the work highly. Creativity is also important when presenting the final outcome, to ensure originality. The aim should be to provide the audience with a new perspective that challenges their existing assumptions. Finally, keeping quality criteria firmly in mind is important both when creating a documentary and carrying out qualitative research; knowing how reviewers/critics will judge your work allows you to reflect on how to achieve those criteria throughout the planning and execution process and when finished.

Putting together a qualitative HCI research production can be an exciting, intellectually stimulating and rewarding experience—where the process is as enjoyable as the product. We hope that now we have taken you behind the scenes, you will be more empowered to plan, conduct, analyse and report a high standard of qualitative HCI research. And that you will enjoy the experience. That's a wrap!

# Bibliography

Adams, A., Blandford, A., and Lunt, P. (2005). Social empowerment and exclusion: A case study on digital libraries. *ACM Transactions on CHI*. 12.2. 174–200. DOI: 10.1145/1067860.1067863. 54, 89

Adams, A. and Blandford, A. (2005). Digital libraries' support for the user's 'information journey'. *Proceedings of the 5th ACM/IEEE-CS joint conference on Digital libraries* (pp. 160–169). ACM. DOI: 10.1145/1065385.1065424. 45

Adams, A., Lunt, P., and Cairns, P. (2008). A qualitative approach to HCI research. In: Cairns, Paul and Cox, Anna eds. *Research Methods for Human-Computer Interaction*. Cambridge, UK: Cambridge University Press, pp. 138–157. 69, 90

Ament, M. G. A., Cox, A. L., Blandford, A., and Brumby, D. P. (2013). Making a task difficult: Evidence that device-oriented steps are effortful and error-prone. *Journal of Experimental Psychology: Applied*, Vol 19(3), 195-204. DOI: 10.1037/a0034397. 62

Anderson, R. J. (1994). Representations and requirements: The value of ethnography in system design. *Human-computer Interaction*, 9(3), 151–182. DOI: 10.1207/s15327051hci0902_1. 64

Arthur, S. and Nazroo, J. (2003). Designing fieldwork strategies and materials. In J. Ritchie and J. Lewis (Eds.) *Qualitative Research Practice: A Guide for Social Science Students and Researchers*, London: Sage, pp. 109–137. 41

Atkinson, R. and Flint, J. (2001). Accessing hidden and hard-to-reach populations: Snowball research strategies. *Social Research Update*, 33(1), 1–4. 26

Atkinson, P. and Hammersley, M. (1994). Ethnography and participant observation. *Handbook of Qualitative Research*, 1(23), 248–261. 68

Attfield, S., Fegan, S., and Blandford, A. (2008). Idea Generation and Material Consolidation: Tool Use and Intermediate Artefacts in a Case Study of Journalistic Writing. *Cognition, Technology & Work*. DOI: 10.1007/s10111-008-0111-6. 30

Attfield, S. and Blandford, A. (2011). Making sense of digital footprints in team-based legal investigations: the acquisition of focus. *Human–Computer Interaction Journal*. 26(1&2). 38–71. DOI: 10.1080/07370024.2011.556548. 10

Barbour, R. S. (2001). Checklists for improving rigour in qualitative research: a case of the tail wagging the dog?. *BMJ: British Medical Journal*, 322(7294), 1115–1117. DOI: 10.1136/bmj.322.7294.1115. 94

BBC (2014). Nature: behind the scenes. www.bbc.co.uk/nature/collections/p00mr6nq (accessed 1st Feb. 2016). xvii

Beyer, H. and Holtzblatt, K. (1998). *Contextual Design: Defining Customer-centered Systems*. Elsevier. 36, 68

Blandford, A. (2014). Semi-structured qualitative studies. In: Soegaard, Mads and Dam, Rikke Friis (eds.). *The Encyclopedia of Human-Computer Interaction*, 2nd Ed. Aarhus, Denmark: The Interaction Design Foundation. Available online at http://www.interaction-design.org/encyclopedia/semi-structured_qualitative_studies.html. xv

Blandford, A. and Attfield, S. (2010). *Interacting with information*. Synthesis Lectures on Human-Centered Informatics, 3(1), 1–99. Morgan & Claypool. DOI: 10.2200/S00227ED-1V01Y200911HCI006.1

Blandford, A. and Rugg, G. (2002). A case study on integrating contextual information with usability evaluation. *International Journal of Human-Computer Studies*. 57.1, 75–99. DOI: 10.1006/ijhc.2002.1013. 40

Blandford, A. and Wong, W. (2004). Situation Awareness in Emergency Medical Dispatch. *International Journal of Human-Computer Studies*. 61(4). 421–452. DOI: 10.1016/j.ijhcs.2003.12.012. 27, 35, 38, 68

Blandford, A., Adams, A., Attfield, S., Buchanan, G., Gow, J., Makri, S., Rimmer, J., and Warwick, C. (2008a). The PRET A Rapporter framework: Evaluating digital libraries from the perspective of information work. *Information Processing & Management*. 44. 4–21. DOI: 10.1016/j.ipm.2007.01.021. 11

Blandford, A., Berndt, E., Catchpole, K., ... and Randell, R. (2015a). Strategies for conducting situated studies of technology use in hospitals. *Cognition, Technology & Work*, 17(4), 489–502. DOI: 10.1007/s10111-014-0318-7. 14

Blandford, A., Farrington, K., Mayer, A., Walker, D., and Rajkomar, A. (2015b). Coping strategies when self-managing care on home haemodialysis. *Journal of Renal Nursing*, 7(5), 222–228. DOI: 10.12968/jorn.2015.7.5.222. 15

Blomberg, J. and Burrell, M. (2009). An ethnographic approach to design. In: Sears, A. & Jacko, J. (Eds.) *Human-Computer Interaction: Development Process*, pp. 71–94. NY: USA. CRC Press. 64

Blythe, M. and Cairns, P. (2009). Critical methods and user generated content: the iPhone on YouTube. *Proc. SIGCHI Conference on Human Factors in Computing Systems* (1467–1476). ACM. DOI: 10.1145/1518701.1518923. 47

Blythe, M., Wright, P., Bowers, J., Boucher, A., Jarvis, N., Reynolds, P., and Gaver, B. (2010). Age and experience: ludic engagement in a residential care setting. *Proceedings of the 8th ACM Conference on Designing Interactive Systems* (pp. 161–170). ACM. DOI: 10.1145/1858171.1858200. 45

Boren, T. and Ramey, J. (2000). Thinking aloud: Reconciling theory and practice. *Professional Communication, IEEE Transactions on*, 43(3), 261–278. DOI: 10.1109/47.867942. 40

Braun, V. and Clarke, V. (2006). Using thematic analysis in psychology. *Qualitative Research in Psychology*, 3(2), 77–101. DOI: 10.1191/1478088706qp063oa. 3, 56, 57, 80, 98

Bryman A. and Burgess RG (1994). Developments in qualitative data analysis: an introduction. In A Bryman & RG Burgess (Eds.) *Analysing Qualitative Data*. London: Routledge. Pp. 1–17. DOI: 10.4324/9780203413081_chapter_11. 2

Button, G. and Sharrock, W. (2009). *Studies of Work and the Workplace in HCI: Concepts and Techniques*. Synthesis Lectures on Human-Centered Informatics, 2(1), 1–96. Morgan & Claypool. DOI: 10.2200/S00177ED1V01Y200903HCI003. 67

Byron, K. (2013). *Creativity in Research. Encyclopedia of Creativity, Invention, Innovation and Entrepreneurship*, 437–447. DOI: 10.1007/978-1-4614-3858-8_9. 91

Calvillo-Gamez, E. H., Cairns, P., and Blandford, A. (2008). Assessing the gaming experience using puppetry. In Bernhaupt, R., IJsselsteijn, W., Mueller, F., Tscheligi, M., and Wixon, D. (Eds.). *Workshop on Evaluating User Experience in Games. ACM SIGCHI*. ACM Press. 47

Carayon, P., Hundt, A. S., Karsh, B. T., Gurses, A. P., Alvarado, C. J., Smith, M., and Brennan, P. F. (2006). Work system design for patient safety: the SEIPS model. *Quality and Safety in Health Care*, 15(suppl 1), i50–i58. DOI: 10.1136/qshc.2005.015842. 93

CASP (2013). CASP Qualitative checklist. Available from http://media.wix.com/ugd/dded87_29c5b002d99342f788c6ac670e49f274.pdf (accessed 17/11/15). 84

Charmaz, K. (2014). *Constructing Grounded Theory* (2nd ed.). Sage. 44, 59, 69, 80

Concato, J., Shah, N., and Horwitz, R. I. (2000). Randomized, controlled trials, observational studies, and the hierarchy of research designs. *New England Journal of Medicine*, 342(25), 1887–1892. DOI: 10.1056/NEJM200006223422507. 88

Consolvo, S. and Walker, M. (2003). Using the experience sampling method to evaluate ubicomp applications. *Pervasive Computing, IEEE*, 2(2), 24–31. DOI: 10.1109/MPRV.2003.1203750. 46

Corbin, J. and Strauss, A. (2015). *Basics of Qualitative Research: Techniques and Procedures for Developing Grounded Theory* (4th Ed). Sage. 12, 27, 69, 70, 91

Crabtree, A., Nichols, D. M., O'Brien, J., Rouncefield, M., and Twidale, M. B. (2000). Ethnomethodologically informed ethnography and information system design. *Journal of the American Society for Information Science*, 51(7), 666–682. DOI: 10.1002/(SICI)1097-4571(2000)51:7<666::AID-ASI8>3.0.CO;2-5. 67

Crabtree, A., Rodden, T., Tolmie, P., and Button, G. (2009). Ethnography considered harmful. *Proceedings of the SIGCHI Conference on Human Factors in Computing Systems* (pp. 879–888). ACM. DOI: 10.1145/1518701.1518835. 10

Csikszentmihalyi, M. and Larson, R. (2014). Validity and reliability of the experience-sampling method. *Flow and the Foundations of Positive Psychology* (pp. 35–54). Springer Netherlands. DOI: 10.1007/978-94-017-9088-8_3. 46

Curzon, P., Blandford, A., Butterworth, R., and Bhogal, R. (2002). Interaction design issues for car navigation systems. In Sharp, Chalk, LePeuple, and Rosbottom (Eds.) *Proc. HCI* 2002 (Vol. 2). 38–41. BCS. 12

Cycil, C. , Perry, M,J., and Laurier, E. (2014). Designing for frustration and disputes in the family car. *International Journal of Mobile HCI*, 6 (2). pp. 46–60. DOI: 10.4018/ijm-hci.2014040104. 16

Denzin, N. K. and Lincoln, Y. S. (2011). *The SAGE Handbook of Qualitative Research*. Sage. 2, 3, 18

Diriye, A., Blandford, A., and Tombros, A. (2010). Exploring the impact of search interface features on search tasks. *Research and Advanced Technology for Digital Libraries* (pp. 184–195). Springer Berlin Heidelberg. DOI: 10.1007/978-3-642-15464-5_20. 39

Dourish, P. (2006). Implications for design. *Proceedings of the SIGCHI Conference on Human Factors in Computing Systems* (pp. 541–550). ACM. DOI: 10.1145/1124772.1124855. 10, 89

Ellis, C., Adams, T. E., and Bochner, A. P. (2011). Autoethnography: an overview. *Historical Social Research/Historische Sozialforschung*, 273–290. 46

Ellis, D., Cox, D., and Hall, K. (1993). A comparison of the information-seeking patterns of researchers in the physical and social sciences. *Journal of Documentation* 49(4), pp. 356–369. DOI: 10.1108/eb026919. 19

Ellis, D. and Haugan, M. (1997). Modelling the information-seeking patterns of engineers and research scientists in an industrial environment. *Journal of Documentation* 53(4), pp. 384–403. DOI: 10.1108/EUM0000000007204. 19

Erdelez, S. (2004). Investigation of information encountering in the controlled research environment. *Information Processing and Management*, 40(6), 1013–102. DOI: 10.1016/j.ipm.2004.02.002. 54

Ericsson, K.A. and Simon, H.A. (1984). *Protocol Analysis: Verbal Reports as Data.* Cambridge, MA: MIT Press. 40

Flanagan, J. C. (1954). The critical incident technique. *Psychological Bulletin*, 51(4), 327. DOI: 10.1037/h0061470. 42

Flick, U. (2009). *An Introduction to Qualitative Research.* Sage. 98

Fry, C. L., Ritter, A., Baldwin, S., Bowen, K. J., Gardiner, P., Holt, T., Jenkinson, R. & Johnston, J. (2005). Paying research participants: a study of current practices in Australia. *Journal of Medical Ethics*, 31(9), 542–547. DOI: 10.1136/jme.2004.009290. 16

Fugard, A. J. and Potts, H. W. (2015). Supporting thinking on sample sizes for thematic analyses: a quantitative tool. *International Journal of Social Research Methodology*, 18(6), 669–684. DOI: 10.1080/13645579.2015.1005453. 30

Furniss, D. and Blandford, A. (2006). Understanding Emergency Medical Dispatch in terms of Distributed Cognition: a case study. *Ergonomics*, 49(12-13), 1174–1203. DOI: 10.1080/00140130600612663. 15, 19, 20, 66

Furniss, D., Blandford, A., and Curzon, P. (2011a). Confessions from a grounded theory PhD: experiences and lessons learnt. *Proceedings of the SIGCHI Conference on Human Factors in Computing Systems* (pp. 113–122). ACM. DOI: 10.1145/1978942.1978960. 12, 71, 80

Furniss, D., Blandford, A., and Mayer, A. (2011b). Unremarkable errors: Low-level disturbances in infusion pump use. *Proc. BCS HCI Conference.* 197–204. http://dl.acm.org/citation.cfm?id=2305353.

Furniss, D. (2014). HCI observations on an oncology Ward: A fieldworker's experience. Chapter 3 of D. Furniss, A. A. O'Kane, R. Randall, S. Tavena, H. Mentis, and A. Blandford (Eds), *Fieldwork for Healthcare: Case Studies Investigating Human Factors in Computing Systems*, Vol. 1. Synthesis Lectures on Assistive, Rehabilitative, and Health-Preserving Technologies. Morgan & Claypool. DOI: 10.2200/S00552ED1V01Y201311ARH005. 36

Furniss, D., Masci, P., Curzon, P., Mayer, A., and Blandford, A. (2015). Exploring medical device design and use through layers of distributed cognition: how a glucometer is coupled with its context. *Journal of Biomedical Informatics*, 53, 330–341. DOI: 10.1016/j.jbi.2014.12.006. 1, 15, 38

Gale, N. K., Heath, G., Cameron, E., Rashid, S., and Redwood, S. (2013). Using the framework method for the analysis of qualitative data in multi-disciplinary health research. *BMC Medical Research Methodology*, 13(1), 117. DOI: 10.1186/1471-2288-13-117. 56

Garris, R., Ahlers, R., and Driskell, J. (2002). Games, motivation and learning: a research and practice model. *Simulation and Gaming*. 33. 44–467. DOI: 10.1177/1046878102238607. 80

Gaver, W. and Dunne, A. (1999). Projected realities: conceptual design for cultural effect. *Proceedings of the SIGCHI Conference on Human Factors in Computing Systems* (pp. 600–607). ACM. DOI: 10.1145/302979.303168. 16

Glaser, B. G. and Strauss, A. L. (2009). *The Discovery of Grounded Theory: Strategies for Qualitative Research*. Transaction Books. 69

Grady, C., Dickert, N., Jawetz, T., Gensler, G., and Emanuel, E. (2005). An analysis of US practices of paying research participants. *Contemporary Clinical Trials*, 26(3), 365–375. DOI: 10.1016/j.cct.2005.02.003. 16

Grbich, C. (2013). *Qualitative Data Analysis: An Introduction*. 2nd ed. Sage. 69, 98

Guion, L. (2002). Triangulation: Establishing the Validity of Qualitative Studies. University of Florida Institute of Food and Agricultural Sciences working paper FCS6014. http://edis.ifas.ufl.edu/fy394. 94

Hallgren, K. A. (2012). Computing inter-rater reliability for observational data: an overview and tutorial. *Tutorials in Quantitative Methods for Psychology*, 8(1), 23. 63

Hammersley, M. and Atkinson, P. (2007). *Ethnography: Principles in Practice*. Routledge. 64

Harboe, G., Minke, J., Ilea, I., and Huang, E. M. (2012). Computer support for collaborative data analysis: augmenting paper affinity diagrams. *Proceedings of the ACM 2012 Conference on Computer Supported Cooperative Work* (pp. 1179–1182). ACM. DOI: 10.1145/2145204.2145379. 55

Hartswood, M., Procter, R., Rouncefield, M., and Slack, R. (2003). Making a case in medical work: implications for the electronic medical record. *Computer Supported Cooperative Work*, 12(3), 241–266. DOI: 10.1023/A:1025055829026. 10

Hayes, G. R. (2011). The relationship of action research to human-computer interaction. *ACM Transactions on Computer-Human Interaction (TOCHI)*, 18(3), 15. DOI: 10.1145/1993060.1993065. 69

Heath, C. and Luff, P. (1991). Collaborative activity and technological design: Task coordination in London Underground control rooms. *Proceedings of the second conference on European Conference on Computer-Supported Cooperative Work* (pp. 65–80). Kluwer. DOI: 10.1007/978-94-011-3506-1_5. 65

Henwood, K.L. and Pidgeon, N.F. (1992). Qualitative research and psychological theorising. *British Journal of Psychology*, 83, 97–111. DOI: 10.1111/j.2044-8295.1992.tb02426.x. 89, 90, 91, 93

Hertzum, M. and Jacobsen, N. E. (2001). The evaluator effect: A chilling fact about usability evaluation methods. *International Journal of Human-Computer Interaction*, 13(4), 421–443. DOI: 10.1207/S15327590IJHC1304_05. 18

Hollan, J., Hutchins, E., and Kirsh, D. (2000). Distributed cognition: toward a new foundation for human-computer interaction research. *ACM Transactions on Computer-Human Interaction*, 7(2), 174–196. DOI: 10.1145/353485.353487. 15, 65, 66

Holtzblatt, K. and Beyer, H. R. (2013). Contextual Design. In: Soegaard, Mads and Dam, Rikke Friis (eds.). *The Encyclopedia of Human-Computer Interaction*, 2nd Ed. Aarhus, Denmark: The Interaction Design Foundation. Available online at http://www.interaction-design.org/encyclopedia/contextual_design.html. 35, 68

Hsu, A. and Blandford, A. (2014). Designing for Psychological Change: Individuals' Reward and Cost Valuations in Weight Management. *Journal of Medical Internet Research*. 16.6:e138. http://www.jmir.org/2014/6/e138/. 1

Hughes, J., King, V., Rodden, T., and Andersen, H. (1994). Moving out from the control room: Ethnography in system design. *Proceedings of the 1994 ACM Conference on Computer Supported Cooperative Work* (pp. 429–439). ACM. DOI: 10.1145/192844.193065. 10

Hutchins, E. (1995). *Cognition in the Wild* (Vol. 262082314). Cambridge, MA: MIT press. 10

Joffe, H. (2012). *Thematic Analysis. Qualitative Methods in Mental Health and Psychotherapy: A Guide for Students and Practitioners*, 209–223. 57, 63, 98

Kamsin, A., Blandford, A., and Cox, A. L. (2012, May). Personal task management: my tools fall apart when I'm very busy! *CHI'12 Extended Abstracts on Human Factors in Computing Systems* (pp. 1369–1374). ACM. 12, 27, 46, 73

Kaptelinin, V. (2013). Activity Theory. In: Soegaard, Mads and Dam, Rikke Friis (eds.). *The Encyclopedia of Human-Computer Interaction*, 2nd Ed. Aarhus, Denmark: The Interaction Design Foundation. Available online at http://www.interaction-design.org/encyclopedia/activity_theory.html. 66

Karlson, A. K., Iqbal, S. T., Meyers, B., Ramos, G., Lee, K., and Tang, J. C. (2010). Mobile task-flow in context: a screenshot study of smartphone usage. *Proceedings of the SIGCHI Conference on Human Factors in Computing Systems* (pp. 2009–2018). ACM. DOI: 10.1145/1753326.1753631. 16

Kidder, L. H. and Fine, M. (1987). Qualitative and quantitative methods: When stories converge. *New Directions for Program Evaluation*, 1987(35), 57–75. DOI: 10.1002/ev.1459. 112

Kindberg, T., Spasojevic, M., Fleck, R., and Sellen, A. (2005). The ubiquitous camera: An in-depth study of camera phone use. *Pervasive Computing, IEEE*, 4(2), 42–50. DOI: 10.1109/MPRV.2005.42. 10, 46

Kippendorff, K. (1980). *Content Analysis: An Introduction to its Methodology*. Beverly Hills, CA:Sage Publishers. 62, 63

Kjeldskov, J. and Graham, C. (2003). A review of mobile HCI research methods. In *Human-computer Interaction with Mobile Devices and Services* (pp. 317–335). Springer Berlin Heidelberg. DOI: 10.1007/978-3-540-45233-1_23. 69

Klein, G. A., Calderwood, R., and Macgregor, D. (1989). Critical decision method for eliciting knowledge. *IEEE Transactions on Systems, Man and Cybernetics*, 19(3), 462–472. DOI: 10.1109/21.31053. 42

Klein, H. K. and Myers, M. D. (1999). A set of principles for conducting and evaluating interpretive field studies in information systems. *MIS Quarterly*, 67–93. DOI: 10.2307/249410. 89, 91

Kock, N. (2013). Action Research: Its Nature and Relationship to Human-Computer Interaction. In: Soegaard, Mads and Dam, Rikke Friis (eds.). *The Encyclopedia of Human-Computer Interaction*, 2nd Ed. Aarhus, Denmark: The Interaction Design Foundation. Available online at http://www.interaction-design.org/encyclopedia/action_research.html. 35, 69

Krueger, R. A. and Casey, M. A. (2014). *Focus Groups: A Practical Guide for Applied Research*. Sage publications. 45

Kvale, S. and Brinkmann, S. (2009). *InterViews: Learning the Craft of Qualitative Research Interviewing*. Sage. 98

Laurie, J. and Blandford, A. (2016). Making time for mindfulness. *International Journal of Medical Informatics*. DOI: 10.1016/j.ijmedinf.2016.02.010. 73

Lazar, J., Feng, J. H., and Hochheiser, H. (2010). *Research Methods in Human-Computer Interaction*. Wiley. 69

Legard, R., Keegan, J., and Ward, K. (2003). In-depth interviews. In J. Richie & J. Lewis (Eds) *Qualitative Research Practice: A Guide for Social Science Students and Researchers*, 138–169. 44

Lewis, J. and Ritchie, J. (2003). Generalising from qualitative research. In Ritchie, J and Lewis, J (Eds.) *Qualitative Research Practice: A Guide for Social Science Students and Researchers*, 263–286. 89, 90

Li, S., Blandford, A., Cairns, P., and Young, R. M. (2008). The effect of interruptions on post-completion and other procedural errors: An account based on the activation-based goal memory model. *Journal of Experimental Psychology: Applied*. 14.4. 314–328. 62

Lincoln, Y. S. and Guba, E. G. (1985). Naturalistic Inquiry. Sage. DOI: 10.1016/0147-1767(85)90062-8. 93

Lipson, J. G. (1997). The politics of publishing: protecting participants' confidentiality. In J. Morse (Ed.) *Completing a Qualitative Project: Details and Dialogue*. Sage Publications. 81

Mackay, W. E. and Fayard, A. L. (1997). HCI, natural science and design: a framework for triangulation across disciplines. *Proceedings of the 2nd Conference on Designing Interactive Systems: Processes, Practices, Methods, and Techniques* (pp. 223–234). ACM. DOI: 10.1145/263552.263612. 94

Makri, S., Blandford, A., Gow, J., Rimmer, J., Warwick, C., and Buchanan, G. (2007). A library or just another information resource? A case study of users' mental models of traditional and digital libraries. *Journal of the American Society of Information Science and Technology*. 58.3, 433-445. DOI: http://dx.doi.org/10.1002/asi.20510. 39

Makri, S., Blandford, A., and Cox, A.L. (2008a). Investigating the information-seeking behaviour of academic lawyers: From Ellis's model to design. *Information Processing and Management* 44(2), 613–634. DOI: 10.1016/j.ipm.2007.05.001. 1, 19, 25, 35, 39, 54, 92

Makri, S., Blandford, A., and Cox, A. L. (2008b). Using information behaviours to evaluate the functionality and usability of electronic resources: From Ellis's model to evaluation. *JASIST*. 59. 2244–2267. DOI: 10.1002/asi.20927. 92

Makri, S. and Warwick, C. (2010). Information for inspiration: understanding architects' information-seeking and use behaviours to inform design. *Journal for the American Society of Information Science and Technology*, 61 (9), 1745–1770. DOI: 10.1002/asi.21338. 1, 35, 39, 54

Makri, S. and Blandford, A. (2012). Coming across information serendipitously: Part 1—A process model. *Journal of Documentation*. Vol. 68, No. 5, 684–705. DOI: http://dx.doi.org/10.1108/00220411211256030. 27, 92

Makri, S., Blandford, A., and Cox, A. L. (2011). This is what I'm doing and why: Methodological reflections on a naturalistic think-aloud study of interactive information behaviour. *Information Processing & Management*, 47(3), 336–348. DOI: 10.1016/j.ipm.2010.08.001. 71

Makri, S., Blandford, A., Woods, M., Sharples, S., and Maxwell, D. (2014). Making my own luck: serendipity strategies and how to support them in digital information environments. *Journal of the Association for Information Science and Technology*, 65(11), pp. 2179–2194. DOI: 10.1002/asi.23200. 26, 65, 92

Marshall, P., Morris, R., Rogers, Y., Kreitmayer, S., and Davies, M. (2011). Rethinking 'multi-user': an in-the-wild study of how groups approach a walk-up-and-use tabletop interface. *Proc. CHI 2011*, pp. 3033–3042. ACM. DOI: 10.1145/1978942.1979392. 16

Mays, N. and Pope, C. (2000). Qualitative research in health care: Assessing quality in qualitative research. *BMJ: British Medical Journal*, 320(7226), 50. DOI: 10.1136/bmj.320.7226.50. 93, 94

McCarthy, J. and Wright, P. (2005). Putting 'felt-life' at the centre of human–computer interaction (HCI). *Cognition, Technology & Work*, 7(4), 262–271. DOI: 10.1007/s10111-005-0011-y. 10

McDonald, S., Zhao, T., and Edwards, H. M. (2015). Look who's talking: Evaluating the utility of interventions during an interactive think-aloud. *Interacting with Computers*. DOI: 10.1093/iwc/iwv014. 40

Mentis, H. M., Reddy, M., and Rosson, M. B. (2013). Concealment of emotion in an emergency room: Expanding design for emotion awareness. *Computer Supported Cooperative Work (CSCW)*, 22(1), 33–63. DOI: 10.1007/s10606-012-9174-2. 10

Miles, M. B. and Huberman, A. M. (1994). *Qualitative Data Analysis: An Expanded Sourcebook*. Sage. 25, 60, 93, 94, 98

Moggridge, B. (2007). *Designing Interactions*. Cambridge: MIT press. 10

Morse, J. M. (1997). *Completing a Qualitative Project*. Sage publications. 98

Nørgaard, M. and Hornbæk, K. (2006). What do usability evaluators do in practice?: an explorative study of think-aloud testing. *Proceedings of the 6th Conference on Designing Interactive Systems* (pp. 209–218). ACM. DOI: 10.1145/1142405.1142439. 40

O'Kane, A. A., Rogers, Y., and Blandford, A. E. (2014). Gaining empathy for non-routine mobile device use through autoethnography. *Proceedings of the SIGCHI Conference on Human Factors in Computing Systems* (pp. 987–990). ACM. DOI: 10.1145/2556288.2557179. 46, 47

Oliver, D. G., Serovich, J. M., and Mason, T. L. (2005). Constraints and opportunities with interview transcription: Towards reflection in qualitative research. *Social Forces*, 84(2), 1273–1289. DOI: 10.1353/sof.2006.0023. 51

Olmsted-Hawala, E. L., Murphy, E. D., Hawala, S., and Ashenfelter, K. T. (2010). Think-aloud protocols: A comparison of three think-aloud protocols for use in testing data-dissemination web sites for usability. *Proceedings CHI 2010*, 2381–2390. ACM: New York. DOI: 10.1145/1753326.1753685. 40

Paay, J., Kjeldskov, J., and Skov, M. B. (2015). Connecting in the kitchen: An empirical study of physical interactions while cooking together at home. *Proceedings 18th ACM Conference on Computer Supported Cooperative Work & Social Computing* (pp. 276–287). ACM. DOI: 10.1145/2675133.2675194. 47

Pace, S. (2004). A grounded theory of the flow experiences of Web users. *International Journal of Human-Computer Studies*, 60(3), 327-363. DOI: 10.1016/j.ijhcs.2003.08.005. 25

Palen, L. (1999). Social, individual and technological issues for groupware calendar systems. *Proceedings of the SIGCHI Conference on Human Factors in Computing Systems* (pp. 17–24). ACM. DOI: 10.1145/302979.302982. 10

Pennathur, P. R., Thompson, D., Abernathy III, J. H., Martinez, E. A., Pronovost, P. J., Kim, G. R., Lubomski, L. H., Marsteller, J. A., and Gurses, A. P. (2013). Technologies in the wild (TiW): human factors implications for patient safety in the cardiovascular operating room. *Ergonomics*, 56(2), 205–219. DOI: 10.1080/00140139.2012.757655. 93

Pidgeon, N. and Henwood, K. (1996). Grounded theory: Practical implementation. In *Handbook of Qualitative Research and Methods for Psychology and the Social Sciences.* 69

Pontis, S., Kefalidou, G., Blandford, A., Forth, J., Makri, S., Sharples, S., ... and Woods, M. (2015). Academics' responses to encountered information: Context matters. *Journal of the Association for Information Science and Technology.* DOI: 10.1002/asi.23502. 25

Portigal, S. (2013). *Interviewing Users: How to Uncover Compelling Insights*. Rosenfeld Media. 40

Preece, J., Sharp, H., and Rogers, Y. (2015). *Interaction Design* (4th ed.). Wiley. 17

Rajkomar, A. and Blandford, A. (2012). Understanding infusion administration in the ICU through distributed cognition. *Journal of Biomedical Informatics*. Vol. 45, No 3. 580–590. DOI: 10.1016/j.jbi.2012.02.003. 38

Rajkomar, A., Farrington, K., Mayer, A., Walker, D., and Blandford, A. (2014). Patients' and carers' experiences of interacting with home haemodialysis technology: implications for quality and safety. *BMC Nephrology*, 15(1), 195. DOI: 10.1186/1471-2369-15-195. 15, 27, 28

Rajkomar, A., Mayer, A., and Blandford, A. (2015). Understanding safety–critical interactions with a home medical device through Distributed Cognition. *Journal of Biomedical Informatics*, 56, 179–194. DOI: 10.1016/j.jbi.2015.06.002. 1, 28, 38, 65, 72

Randall, D. and Rouncefield, M. (2013). Ethnography. In: Soegaard, Mads and Dam, Rikke Friis (eds.). *The Encyclopedia of Human-Computer Interaction*, 2nd Ed. Aarhus, Denmark: The Interaction Design Foundation. Available online at http://www.interaction-design.org/encyclopedia/ethnography.html. 28, 64

Randell, R., Ruddle, R. A., Mello-Thoms, C., Thomas, R. G., Quirke, P., and Treanor, D. (2013). Virtual reality microscope versus conventional microscope regarding time to diagnosis: an experimental study. *Histopathology*, 62(2), 351–358. DOI: 10.1111/j.1365-2559.2012.04323.x. 28

Reason, P. and Bradbury, H. (Eds.). (2001). *Handbook of Action Research: Participative Inquiry and Practice*. Sage. 69

Rochlin, G. (1999). Safe operation as a social construct. Ergonomics. 42.11. 1549–1560. DOI: 10.1080/001401399184884. 80

Rode, J. A., Toye, E. F., and Blackwell, A. F. (2004). The fuzzy felt ethnography—understanding the programming patterns of domestic appliances. *Personal and Ubiquitous Computing*, 8(3-4), 161–176. DOI: 10.1007/s00779-004-0272-0. 35

Rode, J. A. (2011). Reflexivity in digital anthropology. *Proceedings of the SIGCHI Conference on Human Factors in Computing Systems* (pp. 123–132). ACM. DOI: 10.1145/1978942.1978961. 33

Roethlisberger F.J. and Dickson W.J. (1939). *Management and the Worker*. Cambridge, Mass., Harvard University Press. 34

Rogers, Y. (2012). *HCI Theory: Classical, Modern, and Contemporary*. Synthesis Lectures on Human-Centered Informatics. Morgan & Claypool. DOI: 10.2200/S00418ED1V01Y-201205HCI014. 14, 69

Rubin, V. L., Burkell, J., and Quan-Haase, A. (2010). Everyday serendipity as described in social media. *Proceedings of the American Society for Information Science and Technology*, 47(1), 1–2. DOI: 10.1002/meet.14504701409. 47

Schneider, H., Hill, S., and Blandford, A. (2016). Patients know best: Qualitative study on how families use patient-controlled personal health records. *Journal of medical Internet research*, 18(2), e43. DOI: 10.2196/jmir.4652. 10

Segerståhl, K. and Oinas-Kukkonen, H. (2011). Designing personal exercise monitoring employing multiple modes of delivery: Implications from a qualitative study on heart rate moni-

toring. *International Journal of Medical Informatics*, 80(12), e203–e213. DOI: 10.1016/j.
ijmedinf.2011.08.011. 25

Shneiderman, B. (2001). *Leonardo's Laptop: Human Needs and the New Computing Technologies*.
Cambridge, MA: MIT Press. 54

Silverman, D. (2013). *Doing Qualitative Research: A Practical Handbook*. (4th ed.) Sage Publications
Limited. 98

Smith, J. A. (Ed.). (2008). *Qualitative Psychology: A Practical Guide to Research Methods*. Sage. 98

Smith, P., Blandford, A., and Back, J. (2009). Questioning, exploring, narrating and playing in the
control room to maintain system safety. *Cognition Technology and Work*. 279-291. DOI:
10.1007/s10111-008-0116–1. 67, 80

Thimbleby, H. (2008). Write now. In P. Cairns and A. Cox (Eds.) *Research Methods in Human–Computer Interaction*, 196–211. 98

Vincent, C. J. and Blandford, A. (2015). Usability standards meet scenario-based design: Challenges and opportunities. *Journal of Biomedical Informatics*, 53, 243–250. DOI: 10.1016/j.
jbi.2014.11.008. 97

Vom Lehn, D. and Heath, C. (2005). Accounting for new technology in museum exhibitions. *International Journal of Arts Management*, 11–21. 65

Wenger, E. (1998). *Communities of Practice: Learning, Meaning, and Identity*. Cambridge University
Press. DOI: 10.1017/cbo9780511803932. 66

Willig, C. (2008). *Introducing Qualitative Research in Psychology*. 2nd ed. Open University Press. 98

Winkelman, W. J., Leonard, K. J., and Rossos, P. G. (2005). Patient-perceived usefulness of online
electronic medical records: employing grounded theory in the development of information and communication technologies for use by patients living with chronic illness.
*Journal of the American Medical Informatics Association*, 12(3), 306–314. DOI: 10.1197/
jamia.M1712. 83

Wolcott, H. F. (2009). *Writing Up Qualitative Research*. 3rd ed. Sage. 79, 98

Wong, W. and Blandford, A. (2002). Analysing Ambulance Dispatcher Decision Making: Trialling
Emergent Themes Analysis. In *Proc. HF2002* (electronic publication). 56

Woolrych, A., Hornbæk, K., Frøkjær, E., and Cockton, G. (2011). Ingredients and meals rather
than recipes: A proposal for research that does not treat usability evaluation methods as
indivisible wholes. *International Journal of Human-Computer Interaction*, 27(10), 940–970.
DOI: 10.1080/10447318.2011.555314. 12

Yardley, L. (2000). Dilemmas in qualitative health research. *Psychology and Health*, 15(2), 215–228. DOI: 10.1080/08870440008400302. 12, 89

# Authors' Biographies

**Ann Blandford** is Professor of Human–Computer Interaction at University College London and Director of the UCL Institute of Digital Health. Her research focuses on the design and use of interactive technology in healthcare delivery, and particularly on how to design systems that fit well in their context of use and for their intended purposes. She has published widely on the design and situated use of interactive health technologies, on how technology can be designed to better support people's needs and on modelling situated interactions. She has supervised over 20 Ph.D. student projects to completion, and around 100 MSc student dissertations.

**Dominic Furniss** is a Senior Research Associate at University College London. He works in Human Factors and HCI, largely in the context of healthcare. His expertise focuses on the evaluation of the design and use of technology in-situ, and understanding how technology enhances and disrupts the broader system it is embedded within. Qualitative research has been, and is, critical to this work. This has included atheoretical approaches using Grounded Theory, and developing novel methods to be adopted and adapted by others in Distributed Cognition and Resilience Engineering.

**Stephann Makri** is a Lecturer in Human–Computer Interaction at City University London, with over a decade of experience in qualitative HCI research. Motivated by big "how" questions of information interaction, such as "how do people look for and make use of information?" and "how do people come across information serendipitously?," Stephann has a passion for gaining a detailed understanding of interactive behaviour and feeding that understanding into suggestions for the design and improvement of interactive systems.

Lightning Source UK Ltd.
Milton Keynes UK
UKOW07f1005240416

272805UK00004B/10/P